RAGS

Use it up
Wear it out
Make do
Do without

RAGS

Making a Little Something Out of Almost Nothing

LINDA AND STELLA ALLISON

Photographs by Tom Liden

A YOLLA BOLLY PRESS BOOK

Clarkson N. Potter, Inc./Publishers NEW YORK

DISTRIBUTED BY CROWN PUBLISHERS, INC.

Rags was edited and prepared for publication at The Yolla Bolly Press,
Covelo, California, during the spring and fall of 1978 under the
supervision of James and Carolyn Robertson. Production staff: Sheila
Singleton, Joyca Cunnan, Jay Stewart, Barbara Speegle, Marcia Smith,
Diana Fairbanks, Pam Frierson, James Koss, and Dan Hibshman.

Manufactured in the United States of America

Library of Congress Cataloging in Publication Data

Allison, Linda.
Rags.

1. Textile crafts. 2. Rags. I. Allison, Stella, joint author.
II. Title. III. Title: Making a little something out of almost nothing.

This book is dedicated to our mother who never threw anything away without a fight.

Contents

Acknowledgments

The authors wish to thank: those who donated shirts and socks, either willingly or unwittingly; those who generously liquidated their linen closets in the name of experiment; those who graciously searched their memory banks and cedar chests for examples and stories from times past; and the rag artists who contributed samples of their work to enliven these pages.

Rag Artists

Rebecca Palmer, Joanne Gard, Lillian Elliot, Marilyn Green, Sass Colby, Mary Robison, Rae Holzman, Mary Jefferds, Nanthalie Franklin, Dorothy Buehler, Elizabeth MacLatchie, Lydia Stutzman, Harriet Burroughs, Lynn Aron, and Jack Pole.

Rag Reprints

Acknowledgment is made to:

Greenwood Press, Inc. for permission to reprint material taken from *Folk Beliefs of the Southern Negro* by Newbell Niles Puckett.

Berkshire Traveller Press for permission to reprint material taken from *Home Life in Colonial Days* by Alice Morse Earle.

The editor of *Poetry* and Frances Shaw's granddaughter, Alice Ryerson, for permission to reprint "The Ragpicker" by Frances Shaw.

Anais Nin's representative, Gunther Stuhlmann, for permission to reprint "Ragtime" from *Under a Glass Bell and Other Stories* by Anais Nin. Copyright © 1948 by Anais Nin. Copyright renewed © 1976 by Anais Nin. All rights reserved.

Duke University Press for permission to reprint material from *North Carolina Folklore*. Copyright © 1964 by Duke University Press.

The *San Francisco Chronicle* for permission to reprint "Making Room for the Elderly" by Bill Workman.

The Museum of the American Indian, Heye Foundation, for permission to reprint the photograph on page 27.

The Smithsonian Institution for permission to reprint the photographs that appear on pages 32, 37, 41, and 74.

Rag Art

Page 42. Mario shirt from Guatemala decorated with a set-in piece cut from an olf huipil. Courtesy of Tienda Ho, Latin American Imports, Berkeley, California.

Page 66. The design for this woolen hooked rug was inspired by a candy dish.

It was drawn by Harriet Burroughs and hooked by her mother, Harriet Wright Burroughs.

Page 72. Geometric hooked rug, circa 1880. Courtesy of Paul D. Pilgrim and Gerald E. Roy of Pilgrim/Roy Antiques, Oakland, California.

Page 88. Red hot mama stocking doll made by the stocking doll wizard, Rae Holzman.

Page 103. Handmade Raggedy Ann and Raggedy Andy. From the collection of Jennifer Sturgill.

Page 106. Patchwork purse made in India. From the collection of Carolyn Robertson.

Page 132. Antique rag doll from Peru. From the collection of Carolyn Robertson.

Page 150. The Christmas shirt so cunningly pieced together by Stella Allison.

Page 166. Appliques from Thailand. From the collection of Joanne Gard.

Introduction

AS A KID I was pretty impressed by the miraculous make over of Cinderella. Amazing, I thought, what a few yards of satin, needle, thread, and a few mice could produce in a pinch. I began to consider the possibilities.

Later when I had acquired some sewing skills, I was again inspired. This time it was the image of Miss Scarlet O'Hara flouncing through the Civil War in finery she had reclaimed from the curtains of her drawing room windows. I set out to work a few miracles myself. With thread and fabric, both found and bought, I tried to transform my plain junior-high-school self into one of those smooth glossy girls in the magazines. The results were not always what I had anticipated, but that didn't stop me — the vision was still there. Along the way I learned that meager materials sometimes produce magic results. *Rags* is about this way of thinking and seeing. It is about the inspired art of making a little something out of hardly anything at all. Much of the information in this book is borrowed from the times when survival depended on making every scrap count. These are the crafts of our grandmothers, who were experts at picking the materials for a rag rug or a rag doll from the ragbag. Some of the ideas are new additions to the salvage arts. And a few originated in other lands.

The common thread that ties this book together is the way that these rag artists have viewed what most of us see as rubbish. They have seen rags as the starting points for some unlikely, strange, and nearly always wonderful creations.

These days, when neither materials nor leisure time is so hard to come by, rag salvaging can be a great exercise for your imagination — and a plain old good time. The sources for rags are limitless. There are secondhand stores, rummage sales, garage sales, unworn stuff in your closet, scraps and notions both new and vintage, and homely old throwaways.

The ways for using rags are many. This book includes crocheting, plaiting, knitting, basketry, patchwork, hooking, as well as straight stitching. Woven throughout the book are tales of ragpickers and bits of lore, letters from rag artists and little-known facts about such things as the origins of pockets and peddlers. There are also some scraps of history, bits of folk art, and even some rag word definitions to inspire you.

A thing that has become a rag has been well worn. It has been lived in and grown out of; it has been loved a lot and worn to death. Every rag has a style of its own and a story to tell. This book is an invitation to reach into your scrap pile and let the rags speak to you. *Stella*.

RAGS

Two rugs from scraps, a crocheted rag basket and a quilt block from Grandma's rag bag.

A crazy chicken coat made from T-shirts past and present.

1935

Linda's jeans backpacked through Europe. The jeans are in shreds but the patches remain. →

A surviving T-shirt from six-year-old Stella's tea party, now an integral part of the chicken coat.

scraps from a sleeping bag factory make soft, floating wind-socks.

A shrunken old sweater and one with terminal stretch from old high school days.

Rag yarn cut from velour, old curtains and sad old T-shirts.

Buttons can be found almost a whe

Grandma's cache of wool came in handy for tying together a quilt.

Single socks can always be found lurking in laundries.

The family who willingly or not provided the scraps of clothing for so many rag projects. A family history recorded in cloth!

Ragbag remnants for covering cloth books.

These big spools of thread were 25¢ at a store closeout. (Rabid rag pickers can never pass up a good deal!)

Badges and insignias can be removed from old uniforms.

Junk stores are good for finding gloves of all descriptions.

Sometimes a great notion will come to you from your sewing box. String up a length of shirt buttons or silky spools on a cord.

Bits of lace from a dress that visited the San Diego Zoo now decorate a sweet-smelling sachet bag.

Brocades, embroideries, or bits of ribbon make rich covers for button jewels.

Short bits of ribbon decorate a shirt.

Little buttons spiff up a match box.

A button necklace that looks good enough to eat.

These old wooden spools of silk twist were unearthed in a dusty corner of a junk store.

Stuffed tubes of silk make elegant neckpieces. Slide on some brass fittings from the hardware store for a bit of shine.

This area good source of silk.

Lace neckbands in the Victorian style.

Curtain rings woven on a ribbon make an attractive neckband.

The future rag artists in more traditional dress.

These ragbag juggling balls bring back lots of memories.

Stella's culotte dress got her sent home from junior high school.

Cotton shorts from a long ago summer saved by Mom for future use.

This dress went to first grade on Linda.

Mom's Sunday skirt is here.

Ribbon pocket stitched from a handful of mill end ribbons. →

Sew up some small stuffed drawings to pin on your lapel. Bright marker pens on satin give them a real shine. →

Seminole patchwork bands on the sleeves of a black tunic make a simple but dramatic, rag creation.

Roll up some tiny roses to tuck into your hair

Give your rings and things a home in this woven ribbon bag.

Odds and ends of rickrack tied together with simple embroidery stitches can decorate any-thing from tea towels to long skirts.

A scrap of rick-rack from a dress that visited the Alamo — summer of '56.

Red velvet for soft slippers was found in a garage sale free box!

survivors from Ivy League days.

Old ties collected from garage sales, junk stores, and gentlemen friends. A lot of these are

The rest were discovered at swap meets and flea markets.

Scarves collected from Aunt Annie's trunk.

1

Rag Resurrection

ONCE UPON a time in a far-off land lived a king. The king was a good and kind man who had for many years ruled his land wisely and well. The old king, however, was a little lonely and a bit worried. He had been lonely a long time, for the queen had died many years ago at the birth of the prince. He had found no one to take her place; though the prince was quite a comfort. The prince had grown up to be a fine and fair lad with wit and strength. He was a good son, and the king was proud of him, even though he was a little inexperienced in the ways of the world.

To tell the truth, the worry the king felt was nothing new. All good and benevolent rulers worry constantly about their kingdoms. The old king looked to the future and knew that his years were numbered. It was important to him that the kingdom be in good order when he died. It was urgent that the prince be married to a suitable young lady.

"Son," said the old king, "do you have any particular qualifications in the way of a princess?" The prince had learned not to be surprised by his father's rather abrupt way of doing things. He answered that he had not really thought much about getting married, but in these matters, he was willing to take his father's advice. His only qualification was that the lady be very beautiful. He was, after all, an inexperienced young prince.

Forthwith a proclamation was issued from the palace. The proclamation stated that on an appointed evening a grand ball was to be held in the palace. All eligible young ladies of the land were to appear in a gown of their own making. The announcement offered details to the effect that the young prince was looking for a consort and that the most cunning needlewoman and beautiful lady would have a good chance of capturing the prince's eye.

A flurry of activity beset the kingdom. Snipping, clipping, and stitching could be heard at all hours of the night throughout the land. Rich materials and rare trims were imported into the kingdom in anticipation of this event. Rumors flew as to which girl was wearing what color. Old rivalries were renewed. Dressmaking secrets were whispered over tea. Advice was offered and much of it ignored. Gossip flew. The whole of the kingdom was in a frenzy — save for one remote and impoverished corner where there lived a poor woodcutter and his daughter. The daughter was beautiful and fair, with more than her share of honesty and compassion. Unfortunately, she had no money to spend on a gown, for her father was only a poor woodcutter and her tiny income from taking in laundry was of no consequence.

Being a realistic lass, she knew that she could not attend the ball in the one raggy dress she owned, no matter how carefully laundered and pressed it was. She had resigned herself to a night at home doing the mending while the rest of the kingdom had a high time at the ball. Secretly, however, she still had hopes. She thought that if she could find a ribbon or a bit of trim in the trash from some of her wealthier neighbors, she might make her dress into something that would at least get her past the doorman. That way she could observe the festivities from some dim corner in the palace. After all, it wasn't every day that the local folks were invited into the royal residence.

So the little laundress begged the old scraps from her employers as she made her way from house to house, picking up the week's laundry. Her collection was a success. She realized that there were enough scraps to make an entire dress. Of course, it would have to be a patchwork dress, with bits and pieces from every gown in town. She set out to sew a gown from all her pieces. And she hoped that her courage would not fail her on the appointed evening when it came time to wear her dress to the ball.

It didn't. She dressed for the ball in the patchwork gown of many colors and shapes — and if the truth be known, the woodcutter's daughter had never been prettier. She even got an approving nod from the doorman at the palace. Through the door she marched into a grand hall that was ablaze with all the finery in the land.

Whispers and giggles followed her through the evening. Ladies pointed and wondered as they recognized pieces of their own dresses in her patchwork creation. They whispered at the audacity of the little laundress who had dared to appear in their leftovers. They cackled over the cakes and pointed over the punch and laughed ever so cruelly as the court musicians played. They gossiped as the prince dutifully gavotted with every lady attending the ball. Their mirth and malice seemed to fill the room when the prince danced with the patchwork laundress. Until, that is, he asked her to dance again. Then once again.

It seemed that the little laundress had worked some magic on the prince, for he was bewitched by the patchwork lady or by her curious dress. He was not really sure which, for he was very young and inexperienced.

The king was delighted. Being old and wise and most benevolent, he recognized her courage and cleverness. He was also quite pleased at the possibility of a princess with thrifty ways. His consent to the match was easily given.

The prince and the patchwork lady were married soon after, to the joy of most of the kingdom — except for the sore losers, that is. And the prince and his lady lived happily ever after.

SEMINOLE PATCHWORK

Using the example of colonial patchwork, the Seminole Indians developed a brand of patchwork that is uniquely beautiful. Originally the Seminoles made handsome applique bands that decorated their clothing in the late 1800s. Then they met the sewing machine and invented a clever way of making patchwork.

Photograph Courtesy of Museum of the American Indian, Heye Foundation

Their designs were at once sophisticated and simple. This kind of patchwork was used for men's and women's shirts and jackets, hats, bags, and baby clothes. The long flowing skirts of the women were worn with a loose over-blouse and thick strands of trade beads at the neck. They were wonderful to look at. Seminole patch fashion developed and changed from the beginning of the century until a few decades ago, when it was almost forgotten. This craft is now being revived and practiced. You can practice it yourself. It is easy to learn and a joy to behold.

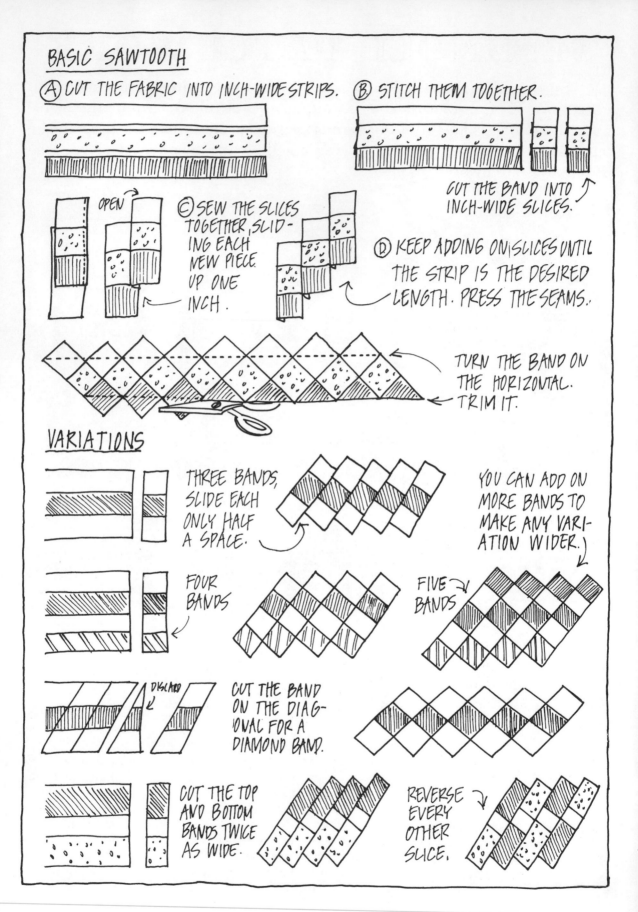

BASIC SAWTOOTH

Ⓐ CUT THE FABRIC INTO INCH-WIDE STRIPS.

Ⓑ STITCH THEM TOGETHER.

CUT THE BAND INTO INCH-WIDE SLICES.

OPEN →

Ⓒ SEW THE SLICES TOGETHER, SLIDING EACH NEW PIECE UP ONE INCH.

Ⓓ KEEP ADDING ON SLICES UNTIL THE STRIP IS THE DESIRED LENGTH. PRESS THE SEAMS.

TURN THE BAND ON THE HORIZONTAL. TRIM IT.

VARIATIONS

THREE BANDS, SLIDE EACH ONLY HALF A SPACE.

YOU CAN ADD ON MORE BANDS TO MAKE ANY VARIATION WIDER.

FOUR BANDS

FIVE BANDS

DISCARD

CUT THE BAND ON THE DIAGONAL FOR A DIAMOND BAND.

CUT THE TOP AND BOTTOM BANDS TWICE AS WIDE.

REVERSE EVERY OTHER SLICE.

THE SAWTOOTH

The basic design for Seminole patchwork is the sawtooth design. It is simply made of three bands of fabric. Choose cotton or cotton-blend fabrics that contrast in color or pattern with one another.

You Will Need

Three different fabrics.
   (Choose scraps that will yield long strips.)
A ruler.
Chalk.

How to Do It

1. Cut strips of fabric using chalk or soap and a ruler to mark and measure them. You may vary the strip sizes from 1 inch wide to 2 or more inches wide.
2. Splice together strips of the same colors on the sewing machine with 1/4-inch seam to make continuous strips. Press seam open.
3. Now cut this basic band crosswise into equal segments, 1 inch wide.
4. Reassemble the segments by slipping each segment up 1 inch and stitching along the side with a 1/4-inch seam allowance. Press seams open.
5. Trim the edges and ends of this new border as illustrated.
6. You can vary this basic design by cutting the strips wider or narrower.

"No man ever stood lower in my estimation for having a patch on his clothes."

   Thoreau, Walden, *1854*

"Men do not realize how great a revenue frugality is."

   Cicero, 45 B.C.

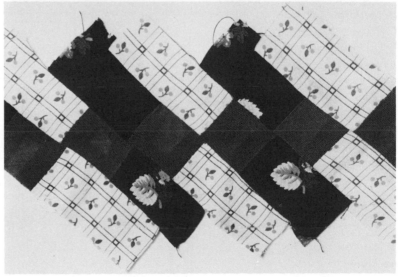

SEMINOLE BAG

Once you've made a strip of Seminole patchwork, you may want to show it off. This simple bag is a quick and easy way to display a small bit of patchwork. Gather up some pieces of calico or plain-colored cotton and play around with the possible combinations of colors and prints. When you've found some fabrics that work, you're ready to sew.

You Will Need

A strip of patchwork about 16 inches long and 1 1/2 inches wide. The basic strip works well.

A piece of polyester batting or mattress covering, 10 inches by 16 inches.

A contrasting lining fabric, 10 inches by 16 inches.

Outer fabric piece measuring 10 inches by 16 inches.

Thread.

How to Do It

1. Fold the outer fabric in half lengthwise and cut it.

2. Splice in the Seminole strip. Pin and stitch it with a 1/4-inch seam allowance. Press the seams open.

3. Pin lining and outer fabric, right sides together, with the batting on the outside. Stitch around the outer edges with a 1/4-inch seam allowance, leaving a 3-inch opening.

4. Clip and turn. Slipstitch the opening shut.

5. Fold lengthwise into thirds to form pocket and a flap. Topstitch the pocket 1/4 inch from the edge to close the pocket.

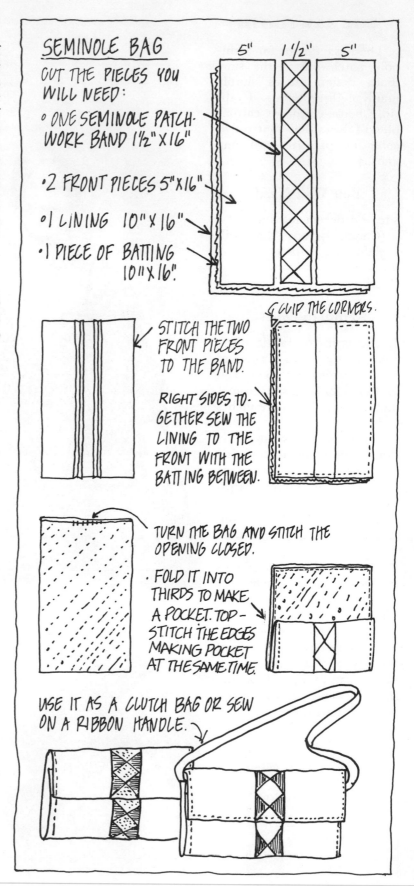

SEMINOLE BAG

CUT THE PIECES YOU WILL NEED:

° ONE SEMINOLE PATCH-WORK BAND 1½" X 16"

• 2 FRONT PIECES 5" X 16"

° 1 LINING 10" X 16"

• 1 PIECE OF BATTING 10" X 16".

STITCH THE TWO FRONT PIECES TO THE BAND.

CLIP THE CORNERS.

RIGHT SIDES TO-GETHER SEW THE LINING TO THE FRONT WITH THE BATTING BETWEEN.

TURN THE BAG AND STITCH THE OPENING CLOSED.

• FOLD IT INTO THIRDS TO MAKE A POCKET. TOP-STITCH THE EDGES MAKING POCKET AT THE SAME TIME.

USE IT AS A CLUTCH BAG OR SEW ON A RIBBON HANDLE.

QUILT LORE

The classic use for bits and pieces is, of course, the patchwork quilt. This cover sewn from rags and scraps has undergone a revival in recent times. So much has been written about the quilt that we have decided to skip the how-to instructions and to touch upon a few other aspects of the quilt. However, if you are hell-bent on making a quilt of your own, check the library. It is sure to have several books with all the details.

Quilting, according to textile experts, comes from the Far East. For a very long time, the Chinese have stitched together layers of cloth to make a warm fabric that hugs the body and retains heat. Patchwork quilting is a more recent idea. Americans like to give themselves credit for the invention of the patchwork quilt. However, English needlewomen object and say that they invented the idea. For centuries, Buddhist monks had been sewing together scraps of brocades that were leftovers from the rich robes of wealthy patrons. The scraps were stitched into hangings used to glorify their shrines. The art of patching small pieces into a larger cloth was probably invented dozens of times in dozens of different ways.

Certainly we can say that American patchwork took a different direction, producing some lively and unique needlework. It is a needle art particularly suited to its origins. What could be more American than a work of art made from scraps — something that could both cheer the eyes and keep you warm at night?

There are a lot of ways to look at a quilt. One of the best ways is from a reclining position with its patchwork surface stretching off in the distance toward your toes, rising and falling over the hills and valleys of your body. Sleeping under a quilt is delicious. Waking up under its colorful surface is a cheerful experience.

A quilt can be looked at like an album of your own personal memories: those red and white polka-dot pieces were from a blouse made for the county fair dress revue; those red checks were a shirt that sat through long hot days in the fifth grade; the faded floral print led the life of a 1950s sun dress that was salvaged from the Goodwill; that white lawn was from a graduation gown. Each piece is an avenue to the past. The stories these bits can tell. Just thinking about them could keep you awake for weeks.

Sometimes you can look at a quilt and read its date from the very fabric. It is a historical document of fashion and technological innovation; an archive of the kinds of colors and cloths America has worn from its colonial beginnings.

PATCH POCKETS

When you can't fit your hands, much less your wallet, into the pockets of your jeans, or when you've got better things to do with your hands, tie-on pockets come in handy. Fashioned after the pockets of centuries past, these can be worn over a skirt or pants.

Nineteenth-century lady's patchwork pocket.

Smithsonian Institution

You Will Need

Assorted cotton scraps for patchwork.
Contrasting fabric for lining.
A yard of 3/4-inch ribbon.

How to Do It

1. Cut twenty-five 2-inch squares of fabric.
2. Arrange the squares into rows of five. Spend some time working out an arrangement that you like.
3. Sew the squares together, a row at a time, with a 1/4-inch seam allowance. Press open the seams.
4. Join the five rows together. Press open the seams.
5. Cut the patchwork into the pocket shape.
6. Using the patched piece as a pattern, cut two linings from contrasting fabric.
7. Pin a lining to the right side of the patch pocket. Mark off a 5-inch line down the center as shown.
8. Stitch around the mark with a 1/4-inch seam. Cut along the line with a sharp pair of scissors. Clip the tips as shown. Pull the lining through the slit and press.
9. Pin the second lining to the right side of the pocket. Using a 1/4-inch seam allowance, stitch around the edge. Clip the curves.
10. Turn by pulling the lining through the slit. Press.
11. With a seam ripper, open the top side seams enough to allow a ribbon to be inserted.

A Short Pocket History

Pockets are cousins to the pouch. A pair of them was tied around the waist and worn under a skirt. Since the fifteenth century, skirts had been made with slits, allowing a lady easy access to her valuables. Not until the beginning of this century did a lady's pockets become a part of her clothing.

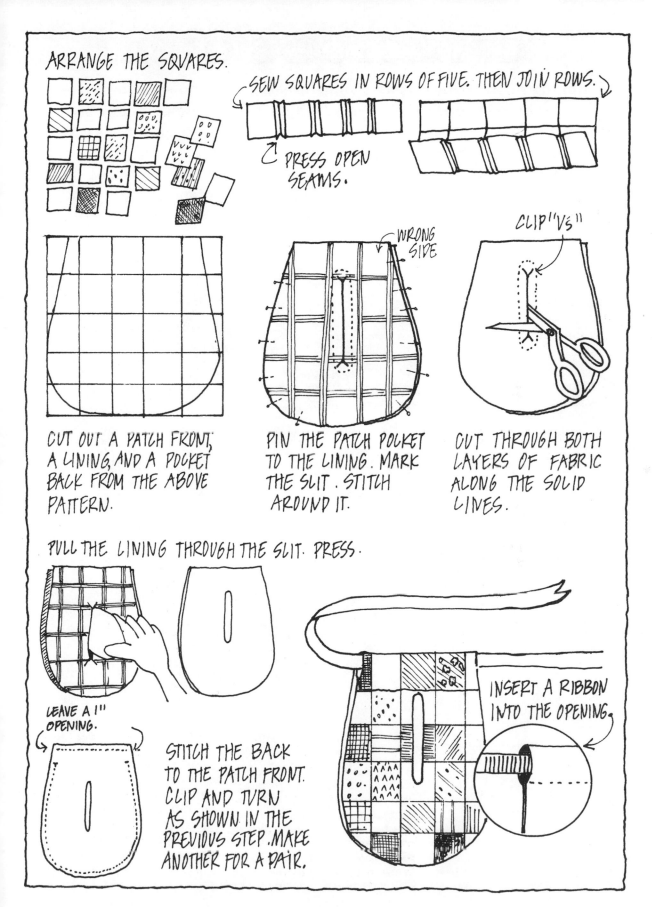

ARRANGE THE SQUARES.

SEW SQUARES IN ROWS OF FIVE. THEN JOIN ROWS.

PRESS OPEN SEAMS.

WRONG SIDE

CLIP "V's"

CUT OUT A PATCH FRONT, A LINING, AND A POCKET BACK FROM THE ABOVE PATTERN.

PIN THE PATCH POCKET TO THE LINING. MARK THE SLIT. STITCH AROUND IT.

CUT THROUGH BOTH LAYERS OF FABRIC ALONG THE SOLID LINES.

PULL THE LINING THROUGH THE SLIT. PRESS.

LEAVE A 1" OPENING.

STITCH THE BACK TO THE PATCH FRONT. CLIP AND TURN AS SHOWN IN THE PREVIOUS STEP. MAKE ANOTHER FOR A PAIR.

INSERT A RIBBON INTO THE OPENING.

33

COLLECTOR'S QUILT

Patching up favorite old pants and shirts is a well-known and much used way of extending the life of old threads. Sometimes these patches are pretty special. If you've invested in patching, you probably know. But there's a point at which holes and tears appear faster than you can patch them. When this happens or you outgrow your patched clothes, think about saving these special patches to build a quilt for snuggling under or as a sort of hanging museum. There are any number of ways you can do this. Use this idea or brainstorm your own.

You Will Need

Salvaged patches.

Fabric scraps of similar fabric for patching.

Enough fabric for a quilt backing.

Enough polyester batting to fill the quilt.

Yarn to anchor quilt top to bottom and a large-eyed needle.

How to Do It

1. Decide on the size of the squares you will need. It depends on the size of the patches you already have. You will need to play with the patches and squares to decide how large and what combinations you want in the quilt. Not every square needs a patch. You may want only half of the squares to sport patches.

2. Now stitch them together with 1/2-inch seams. Press the seams open as you go.

3. When you have finished the top piece of the quilt, lay it on top of the batting and lining fabric. Measure and cut equal-size pieces of each.

4. Pin quilt top and lining, right sides together, with the batting atop the wrong side. Stitch 1/2 inch all the way *continued on page 36*

Quilting, a Miracle of Tedious Work

The amount of labor, of careful fitting, neat piecing, and elaborate quilting, the thousands of stitches that went into one of these patchwork quilts are today almost too painful to regard. Women reveled in intricate and difficult patchwork; they eagerly exchanged patterns with one another; they talked over designs, and admired pretty bits of calico, and pondered what combinations to make, with far more zest than women ever discuss art or examine high art specimens today.

Alice Morse Earle,
Home Life in Colonial Days

PATCHES CAN BE COLLECTED
FROM ALL SORTS OF PLACES.

FIND SOME
PATCHES OR
SEW PIECES
TO PATCH-
SIZE BACKS.

ASSEMBLE THE
PATCHES INTO A
QUILT-SIZE
PIECE.

PRESS SEAMS.

LAY THE TOP ON A
LAYER OF BATTING
AND LINING.

STITCH AROUND THE
OUTSIDE EDGE. CLIP
THE CORNERS.

TURN IT RIGHT
SIDE OUT. SEW
THE OPENING SHUT.

FINISH THE
QUILT WITH
TIES.

VARIATION: YOU CAN SEW
BANDS OF PLAIN COLOR
BETWEEN THE PATCHES.

TO MAKE TIES

SQUARE
KNOT →

SEW THROUGH
ALL LAYERS
WITH HEAVY
THREAD OR YARN.

TIE A SQUARE KNOT.
THEN CLIP THE ENDS.

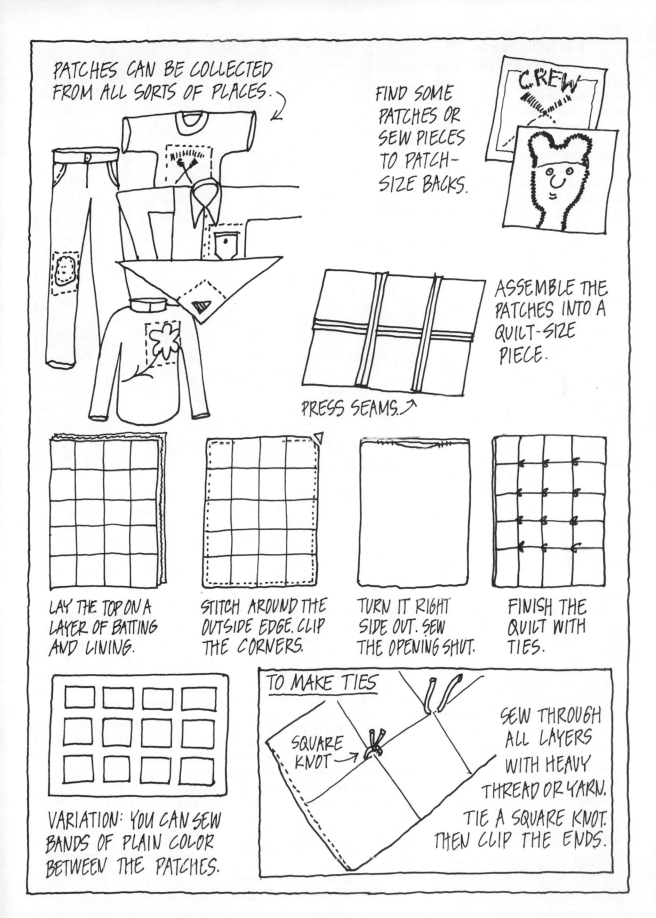

35

The Quilting Bee

The quilt-pattern was gloriously drawn in oak leaves, done in indigo; and soon all the company, young and old, were passing busy fingers over it, and conversation went on briskly.

Cerinthy Ann contrived to produce an agreeable electric shock by declaring that for her part she never could see into it, how any girl could marry a minister; that she should as soon think of setting up housekeeping in a meeting house.

"Oh, Cerinthy Ann!" exclaimed her mother, "how can you go on so?"

"It's a fact," said the adventurous damsel; "now other men let you have some peace, but a minister's always around your feet."

"So you think the less you see of a husband, the better?" said one of the ladies.

"Just my views," said Cerinthy Ann, giving a decided snip to her thread with her scissors . . ."

Thus the day was spent in friendly gossip as they quilted and rolled and talked and laughed . . .

The husbands, brothers, and lovers had come in, and the scene was redolent of gayety.

Groups of young men and maidens chatted together, and all the gallantries of the times were enacted. Serious

matrons commented on the cake, and told each other high and particular secrets in the culinary art, which they drew from remote family archives. One might have learned in that instructive assembly how best to keep moths out of blankets; how to make fritters of Indian corn indistinguishable from oysters; how to bring up babies by hand; how to mend a cracked teapot; how to take out grease from a brocade; how to reconcile absolute decrees with free will; how to make five yards of cloth answer the purpose of six; and how to put down the Democratic party. All were busy, earnest, and certain, just as a swarm of men and women, old and young, are in 1859.

Harriet Beecher Stowe,
The Minister's Wooing

continued from page 34
around the quilt, leaving an opening large enough to turn it inside out. Turn inside out and stitch the opening shut.
5. Anchor the top to the bottom by running yarn through each square at regular intervals and tying the yarn ends together.

More Quilt Lore

It was like listening to a story to hear an old lady describe a quilt into which she had worked pieces of "my daughter's wedding gown," and "my son's cloak." The quilt was replete with memories, for part of the silk bonnet worn at her son's wedding was lovingly stitched into it, and the creamy portions of ivory satin were remnants of her own wedding gown.

Mabel Tuke Priestman,
Handicrafts in the Home

The photograph on the opposite page is of the "Centennial Quilt." The design of this quilt incorporates printed patches which include flags, coats of arms, patriotic portraits, and the Declaration of Independence complete with signatures.

Quilts came into being for many reasons. They often have histories that are highly personal. They might mark a special event in a person's life or commemorate a special person. Engagements, marriages, new babies, farewells, and fund raisers are all reasons for the making of a quilt. Perhaps you have a quilt that has a history of special significance.

Mrs. Austin Ernest made a quilt from the bunting used to decorate the stand at a political rally organized by her husband. Perhaps she was a woman moved by politics or knew a great man when she heard him speak. There is the possibility that she was just plain thrifty. Whatever the reason, today her quilt is valued as a bit of historic memorabilia because it once graced the platform of Abraham Lincoln.

Quilts can be looked at as blankets, treasures, or historical documents. Regardless of their designs, they take on associations and histories and tell stories. It is no wonder that quilts have often been called "museums without walls."

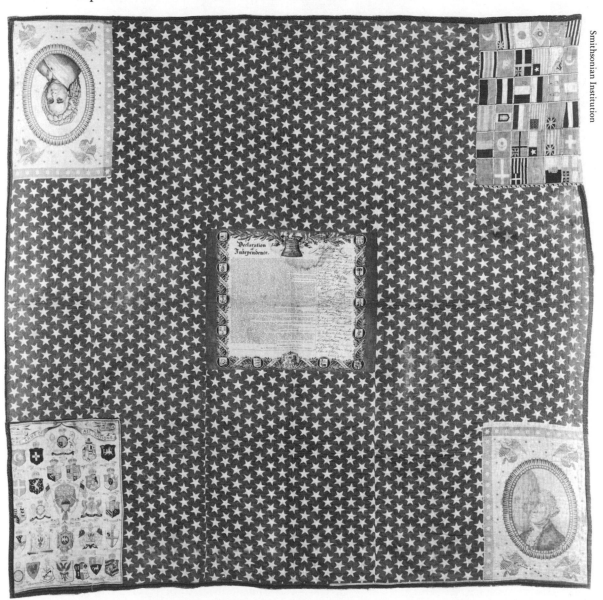

Smithsonian Institution

APPLIQUE

Cloth lends itself well to making pictures and designs. Since it already has color and texture, all you have to do is cut and shape it. Satiny, lumpy, nubby, velvety, furry, fuzzy—compare pieces for texture and allow your imagination to guide your scissors and designs. What sort of scraps have you got in your ragbag? Bits of ribbon? Scraps of an old fur? Metallic fabric scraps? Tattered silks?

Ribbon bits might become a whole kingdom's worth of banners on a fantasy castle. Fur might become a woolly beast. You might find a school of fish in some silver lame, or a tropical bird might emerge from silk. The exciting thing about cloth paintings is that once you establish rapport with your attraction to the fabric, you can build a whole fantasy around it.

Inspirations for the art of applique are the famous vestments of Henri Matisse, molas of the San Blas Indians (this is a kind of reverse applique technique), kids' drawings, or ethnic paper cutouts.

Applique Techniques

Always use fine- to medium-weave fabric.

When cutting shapes, allow for a 1/4-inch margin to turn under on the outer edges.

Preshrink fabric if you are going to be washing it.

You Will Need

Sharp scissors.
Needle and basting thread.
Assorted fabrics.
A straight stitch or zigzag sewing machine.
Straight pins.
Polyester batting (optional).

Ragman's Reward

Foul with dirt are the rags which thy lean horse drags along, but the running water shall one day wash them clean; the rending wheels shall come forth as paper fairer than white lawn.

So with thee poor pillawer: one day thou wilt leave thy corpse and tattered rags in a road-side ditch, but thy soul will fly forth white and fair, and the angels will bear it away to Paradise.

The poor ragman gathers up the foul and tattered rags, and they become the tablets on which are written the wisdom of man and the truth of God; and he that gathers up the lost and the forsaken in this world, and renders them useful and honest members of society, shall in no ways lose his reward.

"Rags and Ragpickers in France"
Chambers's Journal, 1833

APPLIQUE PICTURES

ASSEMBLE A LOT OF SCRAPS FOR AN APPLIQUE PICTURE. THE MORE COLORS AND PATTERNS THE BETTER.

DECIDE ON THE DESIGN. → DRAW IT ON PAPER, OR MAKE A TRACING OF SOMETHING YOU LIKE.

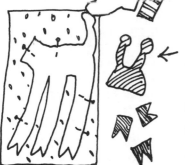

← CUT OUT THE PATTERN PIECES FROM FABRIC. EXPERIMENT UNTIL YOU GET THE RIGHT COLOR AND TEXTURE.

PIN THE PIECES ONTO A BACKGROUND FABRIC. (SOLID COLORS USUALLY LOOK BEST.) STITCH THEM IN PLACE USING STRAIGHT OR ZIGZAG STITCHES. USE ZIGZAG IF YOU WANT A WASHABLE APPLIQUE PICTURE

Needlework Neighbors

I said a few summers ago to a farmer's wife who lived on the outskirts of a small New England hill-village; "Your home is very beautiful. From every window the view is perfect." She answered quickly: "Yes but it's awful lonely for me, for I was born in Worcester; still I don't mind as long as we have plenty of quiltings." In answer to my questions she told me that the previous winter she had "kept count," and she had helped at twenty-eight "regular" quiltings, besides her own home patchwork and quiltmaking, and much informal help of neighbors on plain quilts.

Alice Morse Earle,
Home Life in Colonial Days

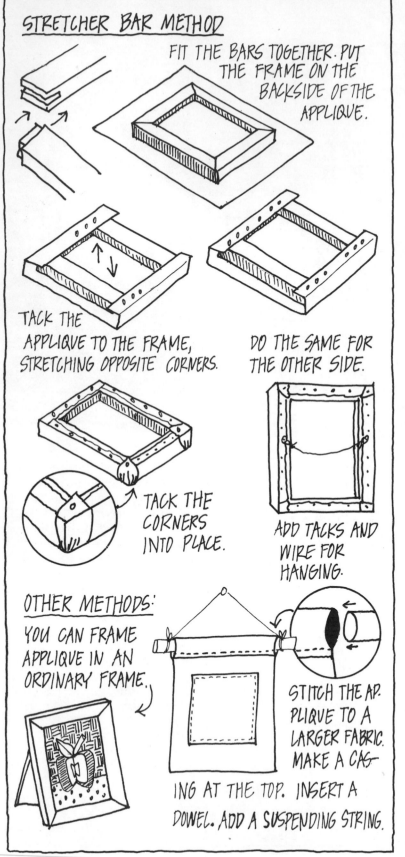

STRETCHER BAR METHOD

FIT THE BARS TOGETHER. PUT THE FRAME ON THE BACKSIDE OF THE APPLIQUE.

TACK THE APPLIQUE TO THE FRAME, STRETCHING OPPOSITE CORNERS.

DO THE SAME FOR THE OTHER SIDE.

TACK THE CORNERS INTO PLACE.

ADD TACKS AND WIRE FOR HANGING.

OTHER METHODS: YOU CAN FRAME APPLIQUE IN AN ORDINARY FRAME.

STITCH THE AP. PLIQUE TO A LARGER FABRIC. MAKE A CAS-ING AT THE TOP. INSERT A DOWEL. ADD A SUSPENDING STRING.

Stretcher Bar Method

You can purchase wooden stretcher bars at an art supply store or paint stores that sell art supplies. They come in many sizes. Choose ones that measure slightly smaller (1 inch) than the fabric to be stretched all around.

You Will Need

Four bars.
Hammer.
Tacks.
Wire for hanging.

How to Do It

1. Fit bars together. They are already prepared, so all you have to do is slide the corners into position.
2. Tack from center out on one side. Then tack the other, taking care to pull the fabric taut and making sure the applique picture isn't distorted.
3. Turn up the remaining two opposite sides.
4. Make square corners (as in bed sheets) and tack them in place. This is a bit tricky. To make them smooth, you may need to cut away some of the excess fabric.
5. To hang, place a tack a third of the way down from either side of the picture top. Wind each end of a length of wire around each tack.

Flowers, Plants and Fishes
Beasts, Birds, Flyes and Bees
Hills, Dales, Plains, Pastures
Skies, Seas, Rivers, Trees
There's nothing near at hand
    or farthest sought
But with the needle
    may be wrought

From an old sampler

Keepsake Framing

When my kid was smaller, he wore a certain pair of overalls day after day until they were soft and worn to holes. He must have put a couple hundred miles worth of creeping and crawling on them before finally outgrowing them. I might have passed them along to another small person, but somehow they've stayed with us. They are perfect for keepsake framing. Do you have some bit of fabric or garment that holds special memories? Think about framing it.

You might frame a fragment of some special cloth in the same way as described in the Lace Framing project. Or simply frame it as you would a photo, with a frame purchased from the store. Another alternative is to actually cut a picture from the cloth you want to frame to create a really personal sort of momento. You can even throw in buttons, buckles, and trims. Use the applique techniques and the framing procedure which are described on pages 39 and 40.

This keepsake picture (above) was presented to our dad to honor his retirement from the Santa Fe Railroad. After receiving it, he said that he wasn't so sure he liked being reminded of his old overalls — but he sure would like remembering that he didn't have to wear them any more.

Grannie sits in her
  oaken chair
The firelight flits o'er
  her silvery hair,
The silent children
  around her sit,
As she pieces her
  patchwork coverlet;
She tells them her
  story of London Town,
And shows them the scraps
  of her bridal gown;
Each fragment there is
  a printed page,
With mem'ries written
  twixt youth and age.

From the old song
"Patchwork"

Smithsonian Institution

41

2

Ragalia

THE TRUE ragpicker has an instinctive talent for conjuring up new uses for old materials. For those of you not intimately acquainted with the cunning of a ragpicker's mind, here is some guiding philosophy on the inventive art of resurrecting worn, tattered, old, or otherwise secondhand cloth.

There are several ways to see a rag. Think of yourself as a salvage cloth-parts collector. When you run across a beautiful piece of lace in a dress, scarf, or linen, or perhaps a beautiful bit of embroidery in an old silk, perform surgical removal with the scissors. Cut out the part you want and discard the remains. Stash it in the treasure box for later or use it as the starting point for a new garment. This is a method used in Guatemalan robes, which combines antique *huipils* and bits of linen embroideries.

Another way to think about a rag is to forget its current function and to focus on what you might make of the fabric. Just

how can you use a damask tablecloth or a funky pair of forties curtains with giant calla lillies? The answer might be to cut a kimono out of the curtains and to make a pair of drawstring pants out of the tablecloth. Woolly blankets make wonderful warm coats. With come clever cutting, a worn old quilt could become a colorful and cozy short jacket.

If one of something won't do or isn't enough, you can always resort to the strategy of piecing things together. A whole fistful of narrow ties opened up and stitched together makes a wonderful skirt. A tea towel combined with some calico from the scrap pile can make a nicely embroidered shirt. A couple of scarves stitched together makes a wonderful soft shirt. And of course there is the tried and true traditional method of patching together little bits to make whole new fabrics. There are a lot of ways to resurrect an old rag, which just goes to show that old rags never die, they just fray away.

SWEATER HATS

You don't have to throw away your favorite old sweater just because it is suffering from a stretched neck or because it is out at the elbows. Take your scissors to it and fashion it into something to wear on your head. Knits can be cut and sewn like cloth. The trick is not to stretch them while sewing and to make sure to finish all the edges so that your project won't develop a case of terminal ravels.

You Will Need

One or more old sweaters (make sure the sleeve will fit on your head).
Needle and thread.
Some yarn.

How to Do It

1. Cut off the end of a sleeve, about 10 inches in length. Slide it over your head to make sure it fits.

2. Turn under the raw edge and stitch it down. If you want to wear the hat folded back, make a 3-inch hem. For a fancy finish, use a contrasting color of yarn and a darning needle.

3. Close the top of the hat by putting in a line of running stitches around the sweater cuff. Pull the stitches tight.

4. Wrap the gathers with the excess yarn and tie it off.

5. Use some fat yarn and a few fancy stitches for a little pizzazz.

Of course the basic hat can be fancied up with tassels, top knots, ear flaps, and decorative stitching. It can be cut long or short, thick or thin — depending on your basic material and your sense of the outlandish. Here are some variations.

THE BASIC HAT

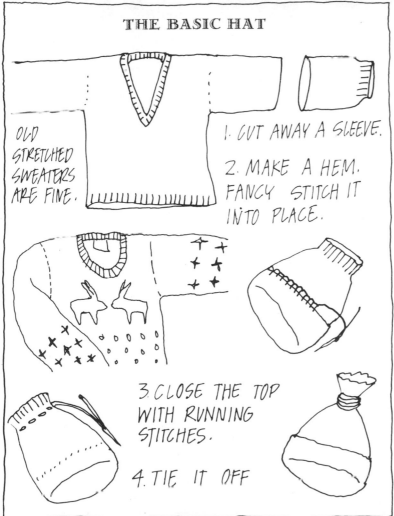

OLD STRETCHED SWEATERS ARE FINE.

1. CUT AWAY A SLEEVE.

2. MAKE A HEM. FANCY STITCH IT INTO PLACE.

3. CLOSE THE TOP WITH RUNNING STITCHES.

4. TIE IT OFF

Sweater Yarn

The sweater is a rough, tough garment with a short history. In fact, the word *sweater* was considered an uncouth nickname for a cardigan. This unfortunate epithet was coined around 1890 by American college athletes. Originally cardigans were the working jackets of the miners in Cardigan, Wales. However, we give credit for the original knit shirt to the fishermen's wives living on the Isle of Jersey.

THE LONG HAT

START WITH A LONG SLEEVE. ROLL IT UP.

STITCH THE BRIM IN PLACE. TIE THE TOP WITH YARN.

TOP KNOT

WAD OF STUFF-ING

CUT A 3-INCH CIRCLE FROM KNIT. SEW A ROW OF RUNNING STITCHES AROUND THE EDGE. PULL IT TIGHT TO MAKE A BALL.

SEW IT ON TOP OF A HAT.

STUFF THE TAIL. TIE IT INTO SECTIONS WITH STRANDS OF COLORED YARN.

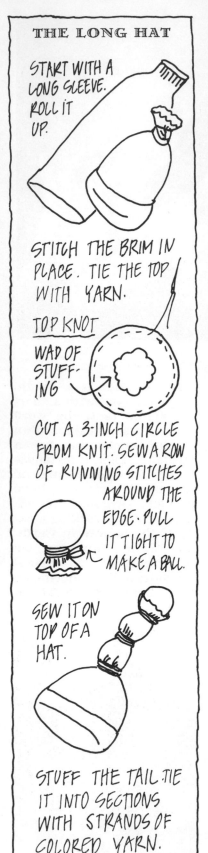

EAR FLAPS AND POMPOMS

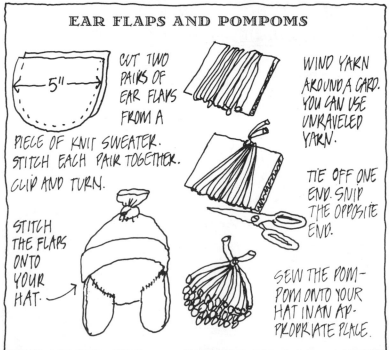

5"

CUT TWO PAIRS OF EAR FLAPS FROM A PIECE OF KNIT SWEATER. STITCH EACH PAIR TOGETHER. CLIP AND TURN.

STITCH THE FLAPS ONTO YOUR HAT.

WIND YARN AROUND A CARD. YOU CAN USE UNRAVELED YARN.

TIE OFF ONE END. SNIP THE OPPOSITE END.

SEW THE POM-POM ONTO YOUR HAT IN AN AP-PROPRIATE PLACE.

THE GREAT HORNED HAT

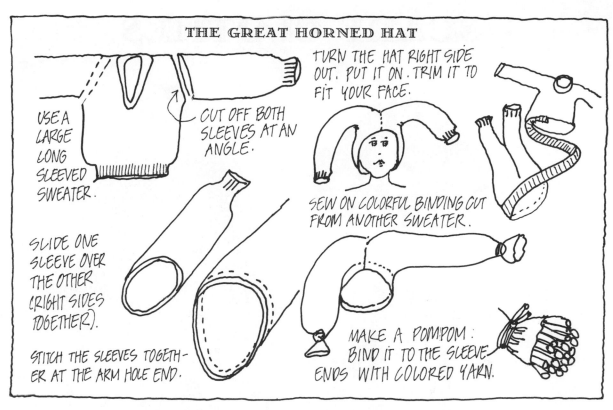

USE A LARGE LONG SLEEVED SWEATER.

CUT OFF BOTH SLEEVES AT AN ANGLE.

SLIDE ONE SLEEVE OVER THE OTHER (RIGHT SIDES TOGETHER).

STITCH THE SLEEVES TOGETHER AT THE ARM HOLE END.

TURN THE HAT RIGHT SIDE OUT. PUT IT ON. TRIM IT TO FIT YOUR FACE.

SEW ON COLORFUL BINDING CUT FROM ANOTHER SWEATER.

MAKE A POM-POM: BIND IT TO THE SLEEVE ENDS WITH COLORED YARN.

SCARF CLOTHES

Scarves make flowing, delicate clothes that are delicious to wear. These clothes are fragile items, not suitable for everyday. But then the results are so elegant, you will only want to wear them on special occasions. You can use old silks with austere patterns or gaudy rayons in bright hues. These clothes can turn out to be as funky as a Tijuana souvenir or as classically beautiful as a stained-glass window depending on the scarves you choose and the way you sew them together.

SIMPLE SQUARE SHIRT

This silky tunic is really a simple square shirt made from two square scarves that are the same size. There's little cutting in this shirt, so it's a good way to use scarves that have special overall designs. If a scarf is very old or fragile, don't use it.

You Will Need

Two scarves measuring 18 inches for a small size, 20 inches for a medium, or 22 or more inches for a large size.

Some fine thread (size 50 will do).

Size 9 machine needle.

Pins.

Enough baby elastic to go around your waist.

How to Do It

1. Put the fine needle on your machine.
2. Place scarves right sides together. Mark off a 6-inch opening in the center top, the opening for your head. Pin and stitch across the top on each side of the opening. These are the shoulder seams. Back stitch to reinforce.
3. Cut a 4-inch slit for the center front neck opening. Hand stitch this with a rolled hem to finish.
4. Starting at the shirt hem, stitch up the side seams, leaving 8-inch openings for the arms.
5. Stitch in a 1/2-inch casing where the waist will be. You can try on the shirt to decide this.
6. Insert the elastic through the casing and stitch the ends together by machine.

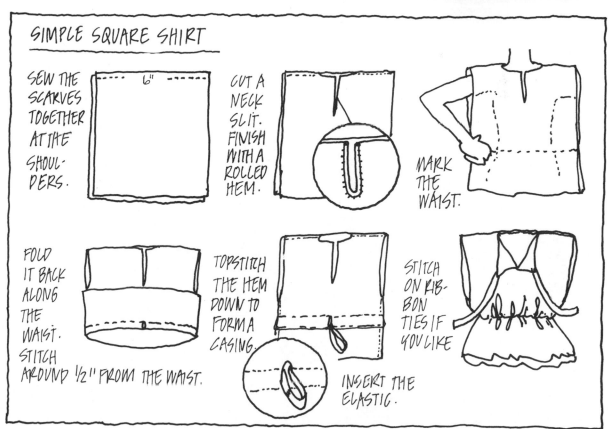

SIMPLE SQUARE SHIRT

SEW THE SCARVES TOGETHER AT THE SHOULDERS.

6"

CUT A NECK SLIT. FINISH WITH A ROLLED HEM.

MARK THE WAIST.

FOLD IT BACK ALONG THE WAIST. STITCH AROUND 1/2" FROM THE WAIST.

TOPSTITCH THE HEM DOWN TO FORM A CASING.

INSERT THE ELASTIC.

STITCH ON RIBBON TIES IF YOU LIKE

LARGE SQUARE TUNIC

There are many ways to make scarf clothes. Let the shape of the scarves decide the design.

You Will Need

Two large scarves measuring 30 inches or more

How to Do It

1. Sew the two large scarves together at the shoulders.
2. Put in the neck slit.
3. Sew the underarm seams.
4. Mark the shoulder to waist length; add about 4 inches. Mark this length all around the tunic.
5. Sew the casing along this line.
6. Add in the elastic.

LARGE TUNIC

THIS TUNIC IS MADE THE SAME WAY AS THE SIMPLE SCARF SHIRT, ONLY IT USES LARGER SCARVES.

VARY THE BLOUSY LOOK BY RAISING OR LOWERING THE ELASTIC.

TUNIC WITH SLEEVES

CUT A SCARF ON THE DIAGONAL TO MAKE SLEEVES.

SEW SLEEVES ONTO THE SHIRT (POINT UP OR DOWN).

IF THE SLEEVE OVERLAPS, CUT IT AWAY. HEM IT.

KNOT THE SLEEVES OR WEAR THEM LONG.

SLINKY SUN TOP

This looks good, feels good, and can be made in the morning before you go out for a day of sunning. Make a few for different occasions. You'll be cool all summer.

You Will Need

One large scarf, about 24 inches square.

How to Do It

1. Cut the scarf in half diagonally.
2. Hem the raw edges.
3. Join the two sides of the halter by knotting them at the corner where the right angles come together. (See the illustration.)
4. The halter is ready to wear. All you do is tie the top two corners together around your neck. Tie the outer corners at the back. This halter top can be tied on in a variety of ways.

The Scarf-Dress Story

One day while I was combing the local junk store for treasure, I found some beautiful silk scarves in a heap of castoffs. Their colors and intricate stained-glass patterns attracted me.

The creative process was in motion. I collected more scarves, some with histories I knew, others I didn't. Eventually they were pieced and stitched together in simple geometric shapes to form a loose dress. As time went on and I wore the dress, some of the older and more fragile scarves disintegrated. I replaced them with new finds. The dress has grown and changed, but that special, magical essence is still strong. *Stella*

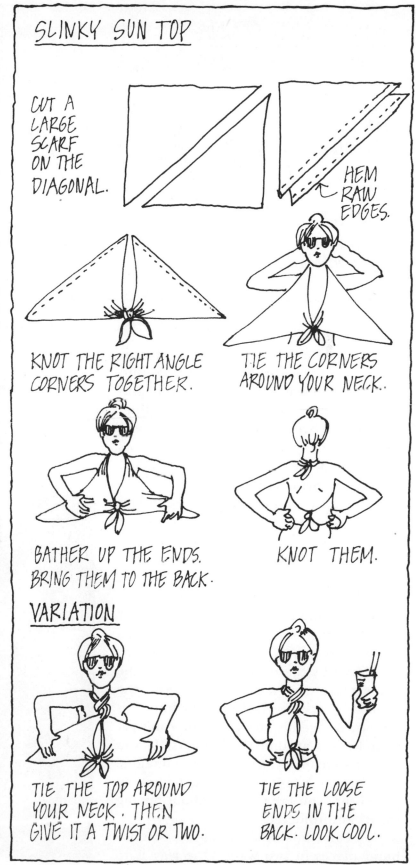

SLINKY SUN TOP

CUT A LARGE SCARF ON THE DIAGONAL.

HEM RAW EDGES.

KNOT THE RIGHT ANGLE CORNERS TOGETHER.

TIE THE CORNERS AROUND YOUR NECK.

GATHER UP THE ENDS. BRING THEM TO THE BACK.

KNOT THEM.

VARIATION

TIE THE TOP AROUND YOUR NECK. THEN GIVE IT A TWIST OR TWO.

TIE THE LOOSE ENDS IN THE BACK. LOOK COOL.

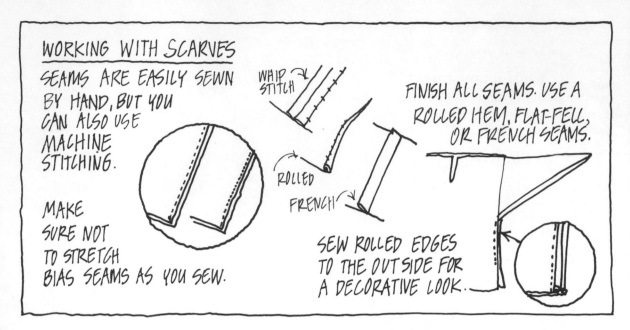

WORKING WITH SCARVES

SEAMS ARE EASILY SEWN BY HAND, BUT YOU CAN ALSO USE MACHINE STITCHING.

MAKE SURE NOT TO STRETCH BIAS SEAMS AS YOU SEW.

WHIP STITCH

ROLLED

FRENCH

FINISH ALL SEAMS. USE A ROLLED HEM, FLAT-FELL, OR FRENCH SEAMS.

SEW ROLLED EDGES TO THE OUTSIDE FOR A DECORATIVE LOOK.

HOW TO USE A JUNK STORE

Part of the excitement of a junk store is the possibility of turning nothing into something. It offers quantities of rags and materials that are cheap and accessible. The things are cheap enough that you have the feeling you can take the scissors to them and, well, if you make a mistake, not much harm is done.

You can fill your closet with objects you never dreamed possible. There is a sense of surprise and a sense of the unexpected. Junking can afford your wardrobe a sense of humor and style that generally isn't possible shopping anywhere else.

But first you may have to conquer your fears of the secondhand store before you can score in one. The trick is not to be intimidated by the dark, dingy rooms, the fellow customers, a sullen proprietor, the swollen racks where everything is crammed together so tightly you can't get your fingers around the hangers. If you are the squeamish type, try not to imagine the last inhabitant of the soiled smoking jacket that you are thinking about buying for its embroidered lapels.

You can think of shopping the second-hand places in two ways. One way is to

look for unusual materials. Think of the merchandise as the starting point. Look for attractive old fabrics, frog closures, shoulder pads, unusual textures, prints.

The other way is to capture complete pieces of costume, clothing with attractive shapes or objects to use or wear for their intended purposes. Dresser scarves, silk scarves, bed jackets, silky night clothes — these things generally demand a bit of altering to make them your own, but they are often well worth the trouble if dressing potluck appeals to you.

And don't forget to haggle. Salespeople at secondhand shops, garage sales, rummage sales, and flea markets are generally willing to talk price with you. If you buy a couple of scarves, ask if you can have a special rate for the lot. Explain that those ties will have to be dry cleaned before you wear them — how about a cheaper deal? And don't forget your sense of humor.

What to Look For

The lot of the ragpicker at the secondhand store these days is considerably slimmer than it was a few years back, before the current wave of nostalgia infected the population. However, it's still possible to happen upon wonderful things.

One way is to look for the items that people aren't looking for yet. Scarves are still to be found. Sewing notions, pearl buttons, and fancy forties buttons are available in quantity. Junk stores have all sorts of odds and ends. Fabric remnants are a good thing to look for. Check the linen bins for laces and embroideries. Don't forget the drapes and bedding. Worn quilts can often be found for very little, and you can cut out the best parts and use them as quilted fabric. Muslin pillow cases, if they are not overworn, are a good source of fine cotton fabric. Clip off the embroideries and monograms to use later as decorations. Ladies' hankies languish in great numbers. Old draperies

are a good source of chintz and period prints. Gloves abound. And if you can figure out a use for toilet seat covers, you will have unlimited materials for years to come.

The best approach to ragpicking is to get there first. Find out which are the best days at the local store, when they haul in the new stocks. And going often is a way to get your pick of the new merchandise. These days the best things don't last long.

What to Do When You Get It Home

Okay, you have brought this thing home. Now remove it from its rumpled recycled bag and think about rehabilitation. First you need to exorcise the junk-store smell before you can actually think about putting it on your own body.

Our mother gave everything a ritual cleaning before it was admitted into the house. First it was left outside in the sun, to kill the germs that might be lurking inside the fabric. A general airing out does tend to get rid of that characteristic musty smell. Then it went into the washer. By this time it would lose a lot of its second-hand stigma. Merely bringing the article into the house and inviting it into your closet to meet your wardrobe will make it seem much more your own.

CHICKEN COAT

    This outlandish coat of many colors is a real show stopper. Basically it's like a 1940s fur chubby; but instead of fur, it sports a wild and woolly covering of T-shirt yarn. From a distance it looks a lot like feathers. It is warm, soft, and somewhat silly and seems to provoke a reaction wherever it goes. Spinsters stare, seamstress types sidle up and ask how it is made, kids want to pet it. It's a great coat for a dull day. And if you're not up to the commotion it causes, you can leave it in a heap on the floor. It makes a nice rug.

You Will Need

Enough double knit to cut a boxy jacket.

A pattern for such a jacket.

At least a dozen T-shirts. Collect them at random or select shades of a single color.

How to Do It

1. Cut all the T-shirts into yarn (see pages 56 and 57).
2. Cut the yarn into 4-inch lengths.
3. Cut out the jacket.
4. Begin to assemble the jacket by joining the front pieces to the back at the shoulder seams.
5. Hem the indicated edges. Turn them under 1/2 inch and machine stitch.
6. Mark jacket with guidelines for sewing on the T-shirt "fur." Use a yardstick and a thin bar of hand soap. (The soap brushes away easily when you're finished.) Make the lines 1 1/2 inches apart along the length of the jacket and the sleeves.
7. Sew the "fur" onto the body by straight stitching over each T-shirt length. Sew the center of every strip along the guidelines. Each strip should touch the previous one.
8. Do this for the body and each of the sleeves. Mix up the strips so the colors don't look patchy.
9. Sew the sleeves to the body at the shoulder seams.
10. Join the front to the back at the underarms. Clip the underarms and turn.
11. Sew ties at the neck if desired. Put them on the underside.

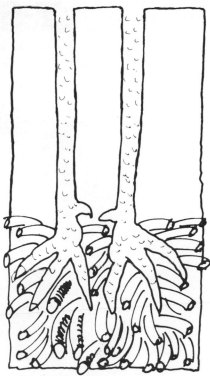

Chicken Coat (above) posing as a throw rug.

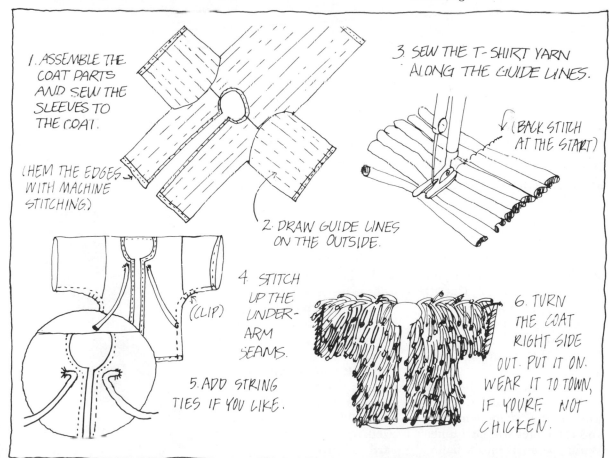

1. ASSEMBLE THE COAT PARTS AND SEW THE SLEEVES TO THE COAT.

(HEM THE EDGES WITH MACHINE STITCHING.)

2. DRAW GUIDE LINES ON THE OUTSIDE.

3. SEW THE T-SHIRT YARN ALONG THE GUIDE LINES.

(BACK STITCH AT THE START)

(CLIP)

4. STITCH UP THE UNDER-ARM SEAMS.

5. ADD STRING TIES IF YOU LIKE.

6. TURN THE COAT RIGHT SIDE OUT. PUT IT ON. WEAR IT TO TOWN, IF YOU'RE NOT CHICKEN.

T-SHIRT YARN

T-shirt yarn is useful stuff. It makes sturdy twine for binding up boxes. It can be colorful enough to tie up a present. Chubby lengths of it can be crocheted or woven into all kinds of things. The best part is that no one would suspect that this fat, happy yarn was once a bedraggled old T-shirt. All you need to transform a derelict T-shirt into yards of yarn is a pair of scissors and some time.

1. First remove the pockets; rip out the pocket stitches or cut off the pockets.

2. Starting at the bottom, cut off the hem. Then cut into the shirt at an angle. Cut a 1-inch strip around the base of the shirt. Continue until the body is one long strand.

3. Do the same for each sleeve.

4. T-shirt yarn has the magic ability to hem itself. Gently stretch the strip lengthwise and the edges will curl under. Wind the strip into a ball.

Not every T-shirt will curl into nice neat string. Only the sort of jersey that is knitted like an ordinary sweater will work. Look closely and you will see up-and-down rows on one side and crosswise rows on the other. If in doubt, cut a sample and try the stretch test.

P.S. If you can afford to be choosy, shirts with no side seams are best, but seamed ones will work. A medium-sized shirt makes 10 to 15 yards of yarn.

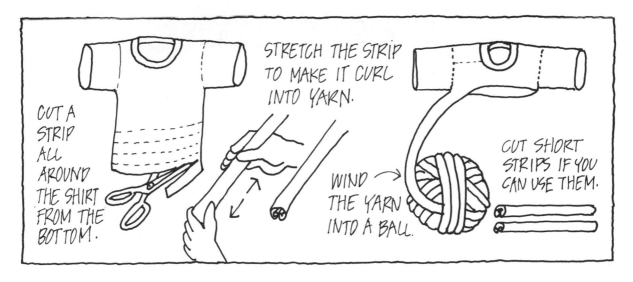

CUT A STRIP ALL AROUND THE SHIRT FROM THE BOTTOM.

STRETCH THE STRIP TO MAKE IT CURL INTO YARN.

WIND → THE YARN INTO A BALL.

CUT SHORT STRIPS IF YOU CAN USE THEM.

JUNK STORE JUNKIE

It used to be that wearing secondhand clothes was something that you didn't talk about. Kids at school would insult each other saying, "You buy your clothes at the Goodwill." Secondhand clothes were not cool in those days, so whenever I heard those words, I'd mentally go over what I was wearing that day. The awful truth was that my mother did sometimes buy things from the Goodwill.

It wasn't that we couldn't afford new clothes. But my mom was an incorrigible bargain hunter. She loved the thrill of the hunt and so scouted fabric stores for remnant bits and occasionally stopped in at the Goodwill to search for "like-new" items. To give her credit, she had a sharp eye for quality and a knack for fitting and remodeling. No one ever accused me of getting my clothes at the Goodwill.

Whenever my mom managed to stop at the Goodwill, I generally stayed in the car slunk down low in the seat so nobody could see me. Only in sheer desperation would I go inside to hurry my mom along. Once the inevitable happened. There I was inside the shop with my mom holding a green and white quilted circle skirt to my waist, when through the door walked Karen Little, one of the most popular girls in my fourth-grade class. I promptly dove between the dresses on the rack, hoping she wouldn't see me. Too late.

My reputation was ruined. Come Monday morning, I was convinced, the whole class would know the awful truth. I was sick. Monday came and went. Nothing happened — a miracle. At the time, it didn't occur to me that she felt the same way and wasn't about to spill the beans.

After that I flatly refused to wear Goodwill clothes. That is until college, when I astounded and confounded my mom by taking trips to the junk stores as part of my vacation-at-home activities. She had no way of knowing that a certain amount of funk and flash was considered chic among artsy college kids.

During these trips I also discovered the Salvation Army, Purple Heart, rummage sales, and flea markets. Some of my most treasured bits of wardrobe are the results of those trips, like my China-silk coat for seventy-five cents, and the leather flier's jacket for fifteen cents, and the brand-new reindeer sweater for a quarter. During all the hours I spent combing the junk stores in my home town, I must admit I never again ran into my fourth-grade friend. It's just as well. Already too many people have caught on to the joys of being a junk store junkie. *Linda.*

57

RAG CURLS

In the 1920s and 1930s, curly hair (Mary Pickford style) was in fashion. If you could afford them you used kidskin curlers to get the look. If you couldn't afford them, you could use rags to curl your hair. The resulting effect was no less rich.

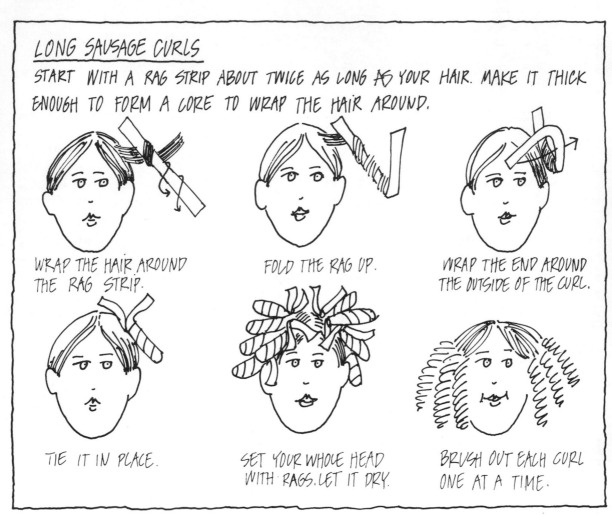

LONG SAUSAGE CURLS

START WITH A RAG STRIP ABOUT TWICE AS LONG AS YOUR HAIR. MAKE IT THICK ENOUGH TO FORM A CORE TO WRAP THE HAIR AROUND.

WRAP THE HAIR AROUND THE RAG STRIP.

FOLD THE RAG UP.

WRAP THE END AROUND THE OUTSIDE OF THE CURL.

TIE IT IN PLACE.

SET YOUR WHOLE HEAD WITH RAGS. LET IT DRY.

BRUSH OUT EACH CURL ONE AT A TIME.

Remembering Rag Curls

Every Saturday or Sunday, the Mexican girls in my neighborhood washed their long hair in washtubs. Most of them didn't have naturally curly hair. But it was the style to wear curls, so they wrapped it in rags. When they took it down, they had those long curls that they would brush each day into all those pretty curls. They were springy enough to last for a whole week.

Kid curlers were what we used to curl our hair. Not everybody could afford them though. If you didn't have curlers, you used rags. For a hairsetting lotion we boiled flaxseed. This makes a kind of clear gel that you can put on your hair.

I never saw my mother with her hair in rag curls. She was the one who put my hair up. Usually we used strips of old white cloth, but using a thick stretchy fabric like socks works better for thick hair. When it was done, I would go outside and play with my hair in rags. By the time I was eight or nine years old, I was putting it up in rag curls myself because, well, you get used to doing it.

Interview with Marie Allison, August 1977

There are basically two ways to make a rag curl. One way is best for short curls; the other is best for long curls. To begin making rag curls, use woven fabric. When you get the hang of them, you might experiment with other types of fabric, like knit strips.

You Will Need

Strips of fabric, about twice as long as a strand of the hair.
Hair-setting lotion if you like.
A comb.

How to Do It

1. Part off a small section of dampened hair. Stretch the section out and holding the rag strip (measuring 1/2 inch wide) at right angles to it, begin rolling the hair around it.
2. When you reach the scalp, tie the rag once. A knot won't be necessary.

How to Do It for Long Hair

1. Holding the strand of hair, begin winding hair about 2 inches from the top of the fabric strip down until all the hair has been wound around.
2. Next, wind the remaining fabric strip up around the hair tightly. When you reach the top of the curl, tie the rag strip ends together.

SHORT CURLS
THESE WILL LOOK LIKE PIN CURLS.

USE 10" RAG STRIPS · DAMPEN THE HAIR.

WRAP THE HAIR AROUND THE RAG.

TIE THE HAIR IN PLACE. A KNOT ISN'T NECESSARY.

SET IT ALL OVER. LET IT DRY.

BRUSH OUT THE CURLS.

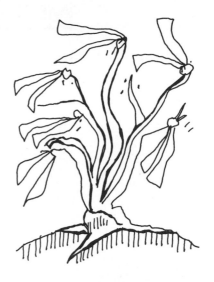

Rag Bushes

In certain parts of the world, the custom of tying strips of cloth onto special shrubs or trees still survives. In more remote times, this custom of cloth sacrifice to cure diseases or other ills was not at all unusual.

The particulars of this ancient custom have been forgotten. Like many folk customs, it seems to have been practiced in many versions. Often a rag bush was associated with a holy well, a place where the waters had special curative powers. Sometimes the bush marked the dwelling place of a spirit. A rag was left behind as an offering in hopes of some positive help. Sometimes a rag represented the diseased part that the offerer had hoped to cure by leaving the sickness behind along with the rag. This accounts for the fact that bushes were sometimes covered with rags. It was believed that anyone touching the clothes could catch the ills that they represented. In some places, pins or buttons were left behind in wells or trees to effect the same cures.

MAGIC WANDS

These are a nifty addition to anybody's costume collection. If you don't have a costume box, you can make them as gifts for any small princess or miniature Merlin you happen to know.

You Will Need

Some satin or taffeta scraps; bits of metallic brocades also work well (old coat linings make excellent wands).
A small amount of stuffing.
A dowel or straight stick about 24 inches long and about 1/4 inch in diameter.
Assorted notions.
A bit of string, metallic thread, or decorative braid.
Glitter.

How to Do It

1. Enlarge the shape you have chosen so that it measures 7 inches in length.
2. Cut a front and a back piece. You might want to use contrasting fabrics for the two sides.
3. Stitch around the outside edges, with the right sides together, allowing a 1/4-inch seam allowance. Leave a 1/2-inch section open so that you can insert the stuffing.
4. Clip and turn right side out.
5. Stuff and whipstitch the opening closed.
6. If desired, paint the stick with enamel or acrylics. Let it dry.
7. Insert the stick into the stuffed section at an appropriate place. Secure it in place by wrapping it tightly with a length of string. Fasten the string with a secure knot. A drop of white glue will help to hold everything in place.
8. Add a button eye to the moon. Tie on ribbons or other whimsies if you like.

MAKE A PATTERN OF THE SHAPE YOU WANT. (EACH SQUARE EQUALS ONE INCH.)

CUT TWO SHAPES. STITCH THEM TOGETHER. CLIP.

TURN AND STUFF. SEW IT CLOSED.

INSERT A STICK. YOU MIGHT NEED TO OPEN A HOLE WITH SCISSORS. BIND IT SECURELY.

GLASS HEAD PINS

SEW ON A POCKET. FILL IT WITH FAIRY DUST (GLITTER).

FANCY BUTTONS

RIBBONS AND BELLS

Costume Box

Kids love to play dress up. There are plenty of grownups who still have enough of the kid left in them to enjoy a change of character now and again too. A costume box is the perfect way to indulge your fantasies. It's good for instant theatricals, home movies, Halloween, or for sneaking around incognito. Besides, it's the perfect place to keep those things you will never wear but can't bear to throw away.

Anything can go into a costume box, but the best things are the ones that are the most evocative — things with a lot of character: Grandpa's military greatcoat, old evening clothes, pointy-toed shoes, satin bed jackets, goggles, swim fins, epaulets, band jackets, junk jewels, wraparound sunglasses, naughty underwear, wigs, choir robes, letter sweaters, long gloves. Things can be found at junk stores and flea markets, but you don't need to look too hard. No doubt a lot of the stuff will come out of your own closet.

SALVAGE SLIPPERS

Conjured up from the scrap heap, these slippers may be worn for dancing and also for footing it around inside. Make them from bits of velveteen, denim, corduroy, old brocades, or what have you. Let your imagination be your guide.

You Will Need

Ribbon, 3 yards.
Some batting.
Old jeans or denim scraps.
Cotton fabric for lining.
Thread.
Some 1/2-inch seam binding.

How to
Make the Pattern

1. Trace around your bare foot on a piece of newsprint.
2. Measure out 1/4 inch from the tracing and draw a line. This will be the seam allowance. Trim away the excess paper.
3. Measure longest distance from toe to heel. Add ½ inch.
4. Now cut a square of newsprint whose sides measure this distance. This paper will be the pattern grid.
5. Fold the paper according to the diagram.
6. Mark crease lines with a marker and ruler to make the pattern grid.
7. Draft the "upper shoe pattern" on this grid according to the diagram.

> "Better to go to heaven in rags, than hell in embroidery."
> *Fuller, 1732*
>
> "Be not influenced by fine clothes, and refuse not him that is in rags."
> *Amen-Em-Apt-Toobl*

MAKE THE PATTERN

MEASURE YOUR FOOT. CUT A PAPER SQUARE WHOSE SIDE IS YOUR FOOT LENGTH PLUS 1/2".

1/4"

FOLD THE PAPER SO IT MAKES A GRID (8 PARTS IN EACH DIRECTION).

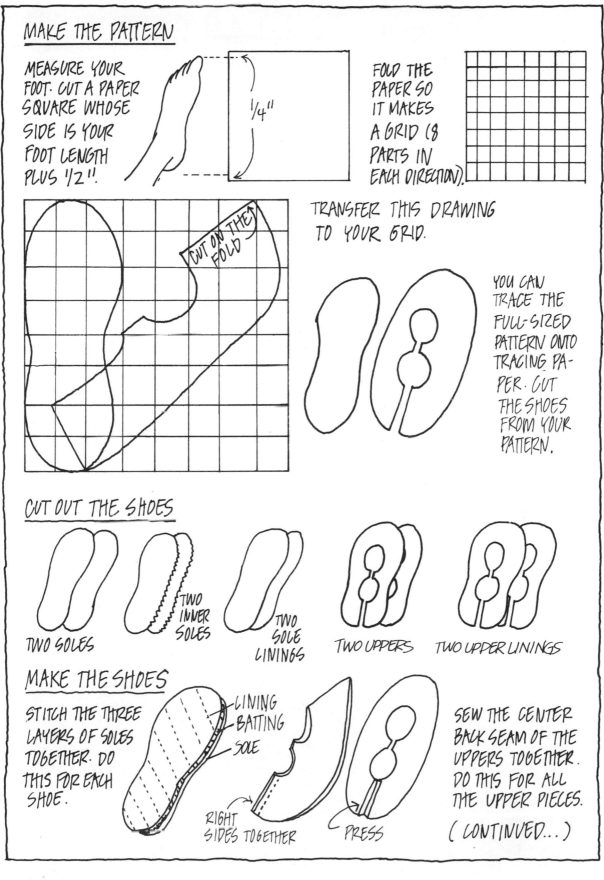

CUT ON THE FOLD

TRANSFER THIS DRAWING TO YOUR GRID.

YOU CAN TRACE THE FULL-SIZED PATTERN ONTO TRACING PAPER. CUT THE SHOES FROM YOUR PATTERN.

CUT OUT THE SHOES

TWO SOLES

TWO INNER SOLES

TWO SOLE LININGS

TWO UPPERS

TWO UPPER LININGS

MAKE THE SHOES

STITCH THE THREE LAYERS OF SOLES TOGETHER. DO THIS FOR EACH SHOE.

LINING
BATTING
SOLE

RIGHT SIDES TOGETHER

PRESS

SEW THE CENTER BACK SEAM OF THE UPPERS TOGETHER. DO THIS FOR ALL THE UPPER PIECES.

(CONTINUED...)

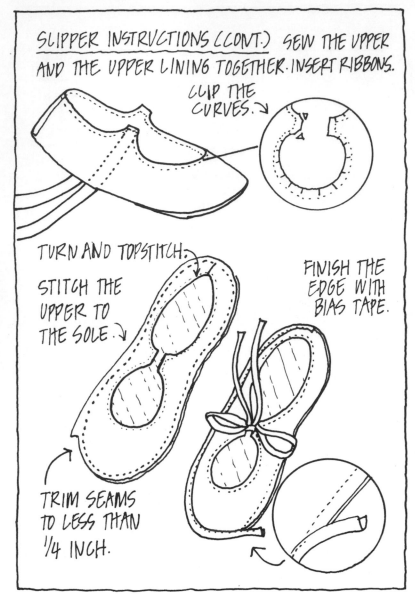

SLIPPER INSTRUCTIONS (CONT.) SEW THE UPPER AND THE UPPER LINING TOGETHER. INSERT RIBBONS.

CLIP THE CURVES.

TURN AND TOPSTITCH.

STITCH THE UPPER TO THE SOLE.

FINISH THE EDGE WITH BIAS TAPE.

TRIM SEAMS TO LESS THAN 1/4 INCH.

Cutting Instructions

1. Cut the ribbon into four equal pieces.
2. Flatten out a layer of batting. Then cut two sole pieces from it.
3. Out of pant-leg pieces, cut two upper shoe pieces and two soles.
4. Cut two upper shoe pieces and two soles from lining fabric.

Sewing Instructions

1. Quilt stitch the lining, batting, and sole pieces together, using rows of stitching spaced 1/2 inch apart.
2. Stitch together the center back seams of each lining and each denim upper shoe piece with a 1/2-inch seam allowance.
3. Pin, with right sides together, and stitch together denim uppers and lining pieces, including ribbon ties as shown.
4. Trim seams at corners and clip seams at curves.
5. Turn uppers to right sides and press.
6. Stitch denim upper shoe pieces to sole pieces. Place seam close to the outer edge.
7. Bind the raw edges with seam binding.

You can cut kid-sized shoes from bits of leftover felt. Trim the edges with pinking shears. Cut hearts into the toes of the uppers to let the lining show through.

Pin-Money

By the term pin-money, is understood a lady's allowance for her own personal expenditure.

For a long time after the invention of pins in the fourteenth century, the maker was allowed to sell them only on the 1st and 2nd of January.

They were so expensive for a long time, that none but the very wealthy ladies could use them; and it became customary to give a certain sum of money to women at their marriage, for buying pins.

On the 1st and 2d of January they flocked to the stores, provided with this money, which was thence called "pin-money."

Since pins have become cheap and common, the ladies spend their allowance on other fancies; but the term "pin-money" still remains in vogue.

Sarah Hutchins Killikelly,
Curious Questions in History, Literature, Art and Social Life, 1886

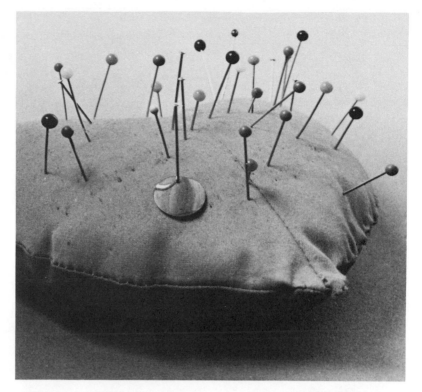

"When you incline to have new clothes, look first well over the old ones, and see if you cannot shift with them another year, either by scouring, mending, or even patching, if necessary. Remember, a patch on your coat, and money in your pocket, is better and more creditable than a writ on your back, and no money to take it off."

Franklin,
Poor Richard's Almanac,
1756

"Mendings are honorable, rags are abominable."

"Keep a thing seven years and you will find a use for it."

Old proverbs

The Second Time Around

In a household in which the family income has to be closely studied, nowhere can more money be saved than in the making over of grown-up clothes for the children. I know one mother whose adaptation of her husband's wardrobe — to say nothing of her own — is marvelous. She claims that almost the only expense she incurs is for paper patterns, on which she stints not at all. Frequently almost the only other expense upon a jaunty little suit is for thread. There is a bag into which go old buttons, good bits of braid, and odds and ends of trimming. The mother has familiarized herself as thoroughly with the dye pot as with the sewing machine, and her prettily dressed children are an object lesson to anyone who would make the most of a limited income.

"Little Economies,"
Good Housekeeping, 1902

Those Old Clothes

In times when communication was poor, folks relied on other means to determine whether their loved ones were alive and well. An object near and dear to the absent person was kept and watched carefully for signs of change. This charm was sometimes a corked bottle of urine or a knife or old clothes. If the object dried up, got rusty, or rotted away, the folks at home knew the person away was not well or had died.

For similar reasons, some people have been known to be reluctant about giving away the old clothes. It was not a question of generosity. Folks felt that it was just unlucky to hand out hand-me-downs to strangers. This unlucky idea came from the ancient fear of witchcraft, when it was commonly believed that a person could do you harm given an article of your clothing.

3

Practical Rags

IN MEDIEVAL times, well-to-do people traveled with tapestries that they would pull out of their trunks when they arrived at an inn. They would use them to cover beds and walls for insulation and to provide warmth and the effect of coziness. These wealthy persons never walked on their textiles. At home it was the same. Floors were, at best, wood or stone. The floor covering was commonly rush or straw matting that was put down and thrown away when it was dirty. Walking on cloth was unthinkable.

The idea of cloth coverings on floors came from the East out of the tents of the nomads whose carpets formed the floors of their portable houses. This idea of cloths to walk on found its way to Europe. It was an immediate success among those who could afford a Turkish carpet. But it wasn't until the machinery to make them was invented that carpets were commonly seen on floors.

Before the invention of carpetmaking machinery, the word *rug* had an entirely different meaning. According to *Webster's Dictionary* 1828, it meant a "woolen cover used for a bed cover." These old-fashioned rugs were an important part of a person's furnishings, and they covered the bed to keep a person from freezing at night when the fire went out — thus the phrase, "snug as a bug in a rug."

In the early 1800s, making rugs out of rags became a common activity among those who were not rich enough to afford a machine-made carpet. Poorer folks reached into their ragbags and found materials to construct their own rugs. Our thrifty grandmothers turned rags into their own versions of luxury for their bare floors. Precious few of those rugs exist now. As objects of practicality and utility, the fate of most of them was death by wear.

Those that have survived are testimony to the creativity of the people who constructed them. The diverse ways in which they were made is amazing. Possibly the best known example of the rag rug is the braided type. Rags have also been knit, woven, crocheted, hooked, and punched or sewn through a base fabric, then shirred to form beautiful rugs.

KNIT RUG

"It was at a suburban village, during a recent visit, that I saw the first tangible example of rag knitting, fresh from the practical hands of an ingenious and benevolent lady, who, upon being asked what she could mean by levying contributions on her friends for every bit of waste material or rag, spread out before my wondering eyes a rug or carpet of many stripes and colors, as picturesque as the blanket of an Indian, and as heavy and thick as a triple-folded railway wrapper.

"'Here,' said the lady, 'is the great absorbent of all your bundles of rags; and I shall be thankful for as many more as you can collect. I mean this for some poor carpetless floor or ill-clad bed for next winter. So, I beseech you, save your rags, and send them hither as fast as you please.'

"My attention was then directed to the materials employed. Every conceivable thing that could be torn into shreds was there — stuff, cotton cloth, list, faded ribbons, velvet, old stockings, and abandoned crinoline covers.

"As a mat for a smoke-room or a summer house, or even for the bedside rug of a bachelor, I can imagine an appropriation of rag knitting to be the very thing. . . .

"I am vain enough to suppose that I have not failed in my efforts to prove that rag knitting may be made a worthy and laudable employment. Indeed, were I to have only directed the attention of the reader to the purpose for which the rug I saw was to be applied, I should feel morally certain that no greater incentive need be given to the industrious and provident, who are glad to fill up every spare moment in those ways likely to be most acceptable to the bounteous Giver of time and all good gifts."

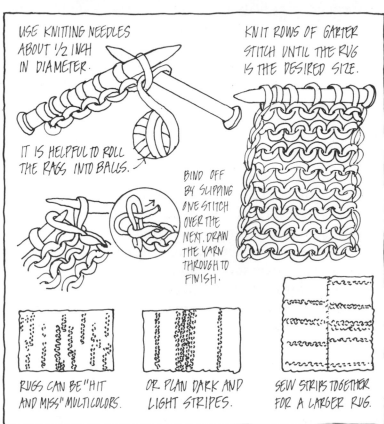

USE KNITTING NEEDLES ABOUT 1/2 INCH IN DIAMETER.

KNIT ROWS OF GARTER STITCH UNTIL THE RUG IS THE DESIRED SIZE.

IT IS HELPFUL TO ROLL THE RAGS INTO BALLS.

BIND OFF BY SLIPPING ONE STITCH OVER THE NEXT. DRAW THE YARN THROUGH TO FINISH.

RUGS CAN BE "HIT AND MISS" MULTICOLORS.

OR PLAIN DARK AND LIGHT STRIPES.

SEW STRIPS TOGETHER FOR A LARGER RUG.

You Will Need

Knitting needles, large ones with 1/2-inch diameter will work well.

Rag strips, the longer the better. Better yet, wind your strips into balls.

P.S. Try to choose colors that will blend together or complement each other. Try to pick fabrics that are similar in content and weight. However, if you want a wild and crazy rug, go ahead and mix denim, velveteen, and brocades. If you want to, try to cut the strips so that they are the same width when folded.

How to Do It

1. Make a slipknot on one of your knitting needles.
2. Cast on as many stitches as you would like the rug to be wide.
3. Commence a row of plain knitting or garter stitch all along the row. When you get to the end, switch the work to the other hand and knit another row. When you get to the end, switch the work to the other hand and knit another row of garter stitch.
4. Keep adding rows until you have the desired size. Try to keep the tension of the yarn even along the way. Thick sections should be knit a bit looser to let them take up more space to allow for an even rug. This sort of rag rug has a width limit of the knitting needle. If you would like a wider rug, consider stitching several sections together.

The description of making knit rugs (opposite page) was taken from an article titled "Rag Knitting," which appeared in Godey's Lady's Book, *1863.*

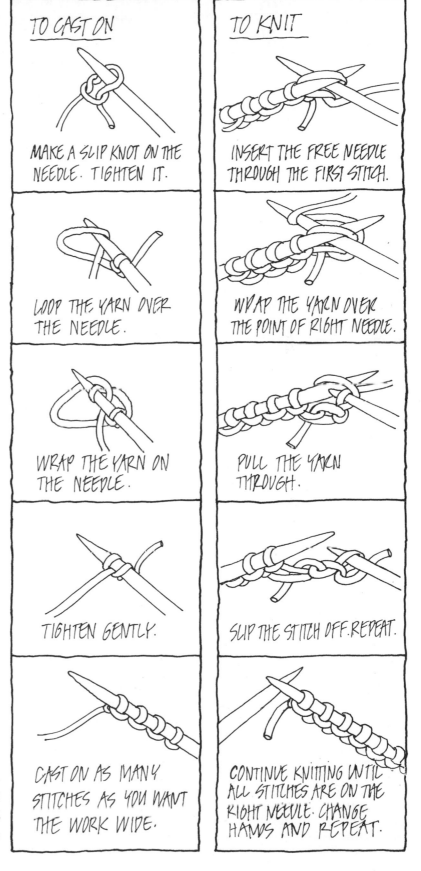

TO CAST ON

MAKE A SLIP KNOT ON THE NEEDLE. TIGHTEN IT.

LOOP THE YARN OVER THE NEEDLE.

WRAP THE YARN ON THE NEEDLE.

TIGHTEN GENTLY.

CAST ON AS MANY STITCHES AS YOU WANT THE WORK WIDE.

TO KNIT

INSERT THE FREE NEEDLE THROUGH THE FIRST STITCH.

WRAP THE YARN OVER THE POINT OF RIGHT NEEDLE.

PULL THE YARN THROUGH.

SLIP THE STITCH OFF. REPEAT.

CONTINUE KNITTING UNTIL ALL STITCHES ARE ON THE RIGHT NEEDLE. CHANGE HANDS AND REPEAT.

RAG YARN

When you are going to knit or crochet with rags, it is handy to join the ends together and wind the strips into balls before you start. This saves having to pause at the end of each strip while you add on the next. Also it keeps things nice and neat so you don't drown in a sea of raggy strips while you work.

How to Do It

1. Tear strips from rags into the desired width. This of course depends on your project. So try a sample before tearing your rags.
2. Join the ends by stitching them together. A sewing machine will hurry this step along. Also try to devise some method for spacing out the colors, so you won't be surprised when all the green falls in one place.
3. Press the raw edges to the center if you don't want a raveled effect.
4. Wind the strips into balls.

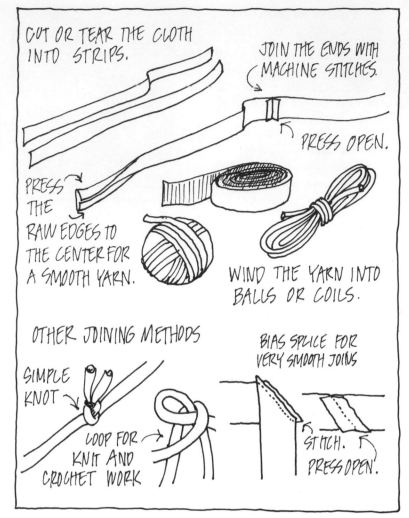

CUT OR TEAR THE CLOTH INTO STRIPS.

JOIN THE ENDS WITH MACHINE STITCHES.

PRESS OPEN.

PRESS THE RAW EDGES TO THE CENTER FOR A SMOOTH YARN.

WIND THE YARN INTO BALLS OR COILS.

OTHER JOINING METHODS

SIMPLE KNOT

LOOP FOR KNIT AND CROCHET WORK

BIAS SPLICE FOR VERY SMOOTH JOINS

STITCH. PRESS OPEN.

Preparation of Carpet Rags

Mrs. Stutzman's pamphlet on the "Preparation of Carpet Rags" was meant to be used by folks who were intending to weave their rags into rugs, but they are good instructions for anyone planning a rag rug of other descriptions. Here they are.

"Hems, tucks, seams, patches, buttonholes, facings, and bindings should be removed, as every hump in the rags means a hump in the finished rug. All materials should be cut or torn across the lengthwise of the goods, never on the bias, as bias rags tear apart. Knitted material should be cut

lengthwise for a smooth weave and crosswise for a rough surfaced rug. All strips that will not stand a quick sharp jerk should be discarded, as they are not strong enough to pay for weaving. Stockings may be cut round and round, but it is not good practice to tear back and forth on sheets leaving a little space untorn at the end of each strip to save sewing. The ends of the strips stick up in the woven rug and give the weaver a great deal of trouble.

"To sew rags properly, the ends where each two strips join should be lapped over for about three-quar-

ters of an inch, the lapped place doubled over and stitched diagonally by machine or hand. When the strips are joined, ravelings should be stripped off and the rags wound into balls about five inches in diameter."

RAGBAG TOUGH LADY

Zuma Francis, 83, is on the warpath against insolent young whippersnappers who monopolize parking spaces needed by the elderly and handicapped at Fair Oaks Community Center in Redwood City.

The self-appointed defender of the center's parking lot has demanded that the city deputize her as a volunteer officer, give her a badge and parking ticket pad, and really turn her loose.

Even without the law's blessing, the spry widow — armed with a 15-pound crocheted handbag that's weighted with boards — has already had a measure of success in confrontations with sassy parking place hoggers.

"This one guy really insulted me," she said yesterday between bites at the center's noontime meal for seniors. "So I swung my handbag and told him, 'Maybe you'd like this where you'd lose all interest in women for four or five years'"

Another time, she said she offered to feed a "knuckle sandwich" to a reluc-tant teenager if he didn't move his car pronto. He did.

Her earthy rhetoric comes from the turn-of-the-century timber country in Washington where she was born.

She is well known at Redwood City, city council meetings as a politician-baiter in behalf of senior causes.

"Why be afraid to stand up to elected officials?" she asked. "They were conceived the same way I was. Their mothers and fathers slept together, didn't they?"

Her request to be deputized was taken under consideration this week by the council. City attorney David Schricker, however, advised that he felt traffic law enforcement was better left to regular police officers because of possible city liability problems.

"I'm not sure if it would be liability because of possible injury to Mrs. Francis," he said. "Or because of possible injury to those she might try to arrest . . ."

© Chronicle Publishing Company
1978

HOOKED RUG

Another name for rug hooking is rag painting. There is probably no better way to describe this kind of rag rug. The results are colorful pictures made from loops of fabric poked through a burlap base. The results have as much soft charm whether you use brand new wools or old scraps from the ragbag.

Credit for the art of rag painting is given to the Egyptian Copts, the Vikings, or sometimes the Anglo-Saxons. Some say that it was brought to America by sailors, who made hooked rugs on their long voyages. Wherever the craft came from, the hooked rug flourished in the seacoast provinces in New England and Canada. No doubt the thrifty aspects of rag painting appealed to the Yankee spirit of these folks, and it was a good indoor activity during the harsh winters. The results made life more comfortable for everyone, whether they warmed the hearth and charmed the eye at home or were sold to supplement a family's income. Hooked rugs became a great cottage industry in those parts of the country.

Of course a craft like rag painting was too appealing an art to remain undiscovered. Folks have hooked rugs all across America at one time or another. It is hard to believe that such wonderful pictures of life in days past were achieved with a simple hook, a piece of sack, and a pile of rags. The fact remains that some of the liveliest and most vivid portraits of times past are painted in rags. And rag painting has lost none of its charm as a pastime in the present.

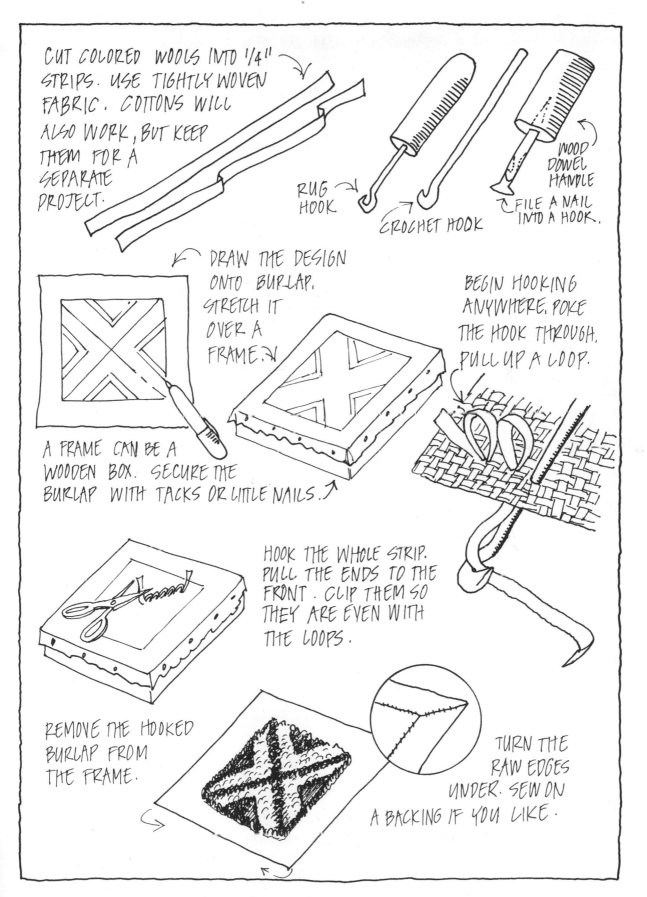

CUT COLORED WOOLS INTO 1/4" STRIPS. USE TIGHTLY WOVEN FABRIC. COTTONS WILL ALSO WORK, BUT KEEP THEM FOR A SEPARATE PROJECT.

RUG HOOK

CROCHET HOOK

WOOD DOWEL HANDLE

FILE A NAIL INTO A HOOK.

DRAW THE DESIGN ONTO BURLAP. STRETCH IT OVER A FRAME.

BEGIN HOOKING ANYWHERE. POKE THE HOOK THROUGH. PULL UP A LOOP.

A FRAME CAN BE A WOODEN BOX. SECURE THE BURLAP WITH TACKS OR LITTLE NAILS.

HOOK THE WHOLE STRIP. PULL THE ENDS TO THE FRONT. CLIP THEM SO THEY ARE EVEN WITH THE LOOPS.

REMOVE THE HOOKED BURLAP FROM THE FRAME.

TURN THE RAW EDGES UNDER. SEW ON A BACKING IF YOU LIKE.

Smithsonian Institution

You Will Need

A piece of burlap for the foundation.

A rug hook or a big steel crochet hook will work fine.

Wool rags of various colors. They should be washed and sorted for color. You might even try dyeing some for a special color.

A large embroidery hoop or a frame is very helpful.

How to Do It

1. Decide on the design and size that you want your rug to be. Cut the burlap to size and draw the design on it with crayon or a felt marker. Leave a border all around. (It's best to start small on the first project.)

2. Cut the wool scraps into strips about 1/4 inch wide.

3. Unless you are working with a very small piece, it is best to stretch your work over a frame, embroidery hoop, or even a box to hold the foundation while you work.

4. Begin any place in the design. Poke the hook through the top of the burlap. Hold the wool strip underneath the burlap with your other hand. Catch it with the hook and pull a loop through to the front. Let it stick up about 1/4 inch. Skip a few threads and make another loop. A little experimenting will help you decide how close together the loops should be.

5. When you come to the end of a strip, pull the end to the topside and clip it off even with loop. Do this for the starting end as well.

6. Lots of rug hookers prefer to outline their designs, then go back and fill in the spaces and the background.

EDWARD FROST,
PEDDLER EXTRAORDINAIRE

Edward Sands Forest was twenty years old in 1863 when he returned home to Biddeford, Maine, from the Civil War. He was so ill that he couldn't return to his old job in the machine shop. Edward needed to be in the out-of-doors, so he took up the life of a peddler. Peddlers often traded in kind, and Frost collected a large quantity of colored rags, which he handed over to his wife. She proceeded to turn them into a hooked rug and Edward became interested in the technique. According to an account in the *Biddeford Times,* 1888, he "caught the fever" and was soon sketching his own designs for hooked rag rugs. He was so good at it that many of his neighbors began asking him for designs.

I got myself into business right away. I put in my time evenings and stormy days sketching designs, giving only the outlines in black. There was not money enough in it to devote my whole time to the business, and as the orders came in faster than I could fill them I began, Yankee-like, to study some way to do them quicker. Then the first idea of stencilling presented itself to me.

Edward took himself out to the barn and began to make stencils from odds and ends he had on hand. Old iron, wash boilers, his machinist's skills, and a lot of Yankee ingenuity produced a set of stencils.

So I began to print patterns and put them in my peddler's cart and offer them for sale. The news of my invention of stamped rugs spread like magic, and many a time as I drove through the streets of Biddeford and Saco, a lady would appear at the door or window, swinging an apron or sun bonnet and shouting at the top of her voice, say, "Are you the rug man? Do you carry rugs all marked out?" I at once became known as Frost, the rug man, and many Biddeford citizens still speak of me in that same way.

My rug business increased and I soon found that I could not print fast enough; I also found it difficult to duplicate my patterns, or make two exactly alike, as many of my customers would call for a pattern just like Mrs. So and So's.

Back to the barn. Edward worked out a way to print entire rug designs with a single plate. Then, ever the inventor, he began thinking of ways to produce the designs in color.

I shall never forget the time and place it came to me. . . . It was March, 1870, one morning about two o'clock. I had been thinking how I could print the bright colors in with the dark ones so as to make good clear prints. My mind was so fixed on the problem that I could not sleep, so I turned and twisted and all at once I seemed to hear a voice in my room say: "Print your bright colors first and then the dark ones." That settled it, and I was so excited that I could not close my eyes in sleep the rest of the night, and I tell you I was glad when morning came so I could get to town to buy stock for the plates with which to carry out my idea. At the end of a week I had one design made and printed in colors.

The colored designs were a great success — so much so that Edward gave up peddling and opened a shop that sold nothing but his designs for rugs. In 1876, Frost sold his business and retired to sunny California with the wealth accumulated from his years as the rug man of Biddeford, Maine.

KNOTTED RAG RUG

This rug can be put down on a floor with either side up. The pile side is thick and furry and a joy for bare feet. The flip side is a smooth textile. With bands of color on the pile side, an interesting optical effect occurs. The effect is like an impressionist painting with dots of color blended by the eye into a multicolor swirl.

You Will Need

T-shirt yarn.
Clothesline cord.
Heavy upholstery-type thread and a needle with a large eye.
A thimble.

How to Do It

1. Cut yarn strips about 5 inches long.
2. Double the cord and tie the ends.
3. Attach yarn strips by folding them in half lengthwise, then looping them over the base cord and pulling yarn ends through yarn loop.
4. Do this, turning yarn pieces up to get a fringe effect. When you've fringed several feet of cord, you may begin to form the rug.
5. Beginning at the end where you started looping on the yarn, coil the cord and stitch the coil to secure it in place with the needle and thread.

Holding the cord taut while knotting the yarn makes the work go more easily and quickly.

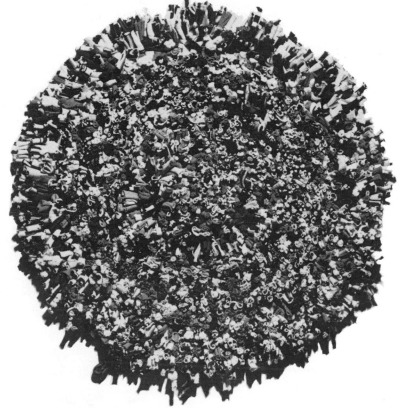

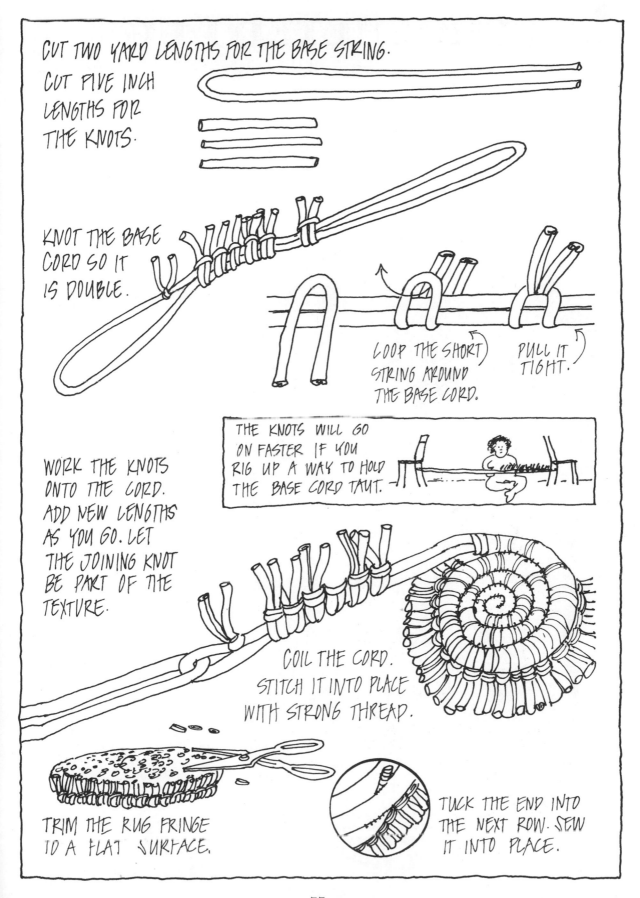

CUT TWO YARD LENGTHS FOR THE BASE STRING.

CUT FIVE INCH LENGTHS FOR THE KNOTS.

KNOT THE BASE CORD SO IT IS DOUBLE.

LOOP THE SHORT STRING AROUND THE BASE CORD.

PULL IT TIGHT.

THE KNOTS WILL GO ON FASTER IF YOU RIG UP A WAY TO HOLD THE BASE CORD TAUT.

WORK THE KNOTS ONTO THE CORD. ADD NEW LENGTHS AS YOU GO. LET THE JOINING KNOT BE PART OF THE TEXTURE.

COIL THE CORD. STITCH IT INTO PLACE WITH STRONG THREAD.

TRIM THE RUG FRINGE TO A FLAT SURFACE.

TUCK THE END INTO THE NEXT ROW. SEW IT INTO PLACE.

CROCHETED RUG

You don't need to be an expert with the crochet hook to transform rags into colorful rugs. All you need to know is a few simple stitches and then catch on to the basic idea of crocheting in circles. At this point you will have learned all the skills necessary to make a crocheted rug. You will find that it is a simple and logical process that can be learned quickly. All you need is some rags, a big crochet hook, and a bit of time to make fat colorful mats for your cold toes.

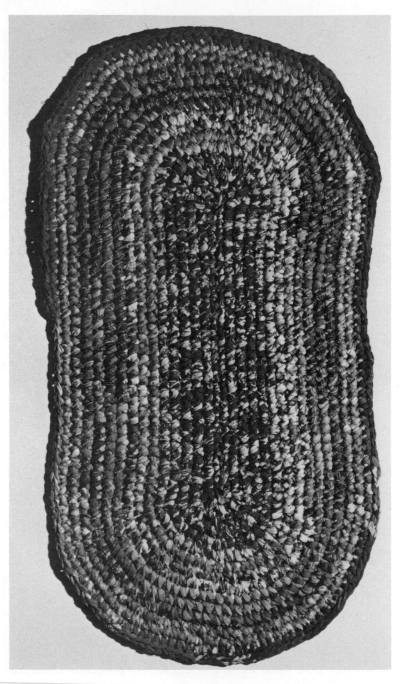

You Will Need

A large crochet hook. How large depends on the size of your rag yarn, which should fit comfortably in the hook.

Also some strips of rags. It will be helpful to do some experiments to get an idea of what hook and rag size you like.

How to Do It

1. To make a round rug, first make a slip knot on the crochet hook with the rag yarn.
2. Make a row of five chain stitches.
3. Join with a slipstitch into the first chain to form a ring.
4. Make two more chain stitches for a total of eight.

Round two:

5. Make two stitches in each previous stitch. This will give you sixteen stitches around.

Round three:

6. Do one increase in every other stitch. This should give you a total of twenty-four stitches around.

Round four:

7. To keep the circle growing in a regular fashion so that it lies flat, you need to increase the stitches in a regular man-

ner. A good way to think of this is to divide the circle into twelve equal parts. Add in stitches along these imaginary divisions. So divide the last round of twenty-four stitches by twelve. You get two. This means you increase at every other stitch on this round.

Round five:

8. Now do a round with no increases. This will keep the circle flat and even.

Round six:

9. You should count thirty-six stitches. Divide by twelve and you will find that you need to increase every third stitch.

Round seven:

10. Do a row with no increases.

To continue:

You can increase by counting stitches and dividing. Or you can increase by eye. You will notice that a previous increase looks like a vee. Make your new increase on top of the second increase stitch of the previous round. Keep crocheting until you have a rug the size you want.

Crocheting with rag yarn doesn't require a lot of precision because the effect is rough and motley. Don't worry if you miss a stitch. And don't be afraid to pull out lumpy bits and rework them to make them smooth.

To Make an Oval Rug

The method for an oval rug is much the same as for a circle. The only difference is that the increasing happens at the curved ends rather than all the way around.

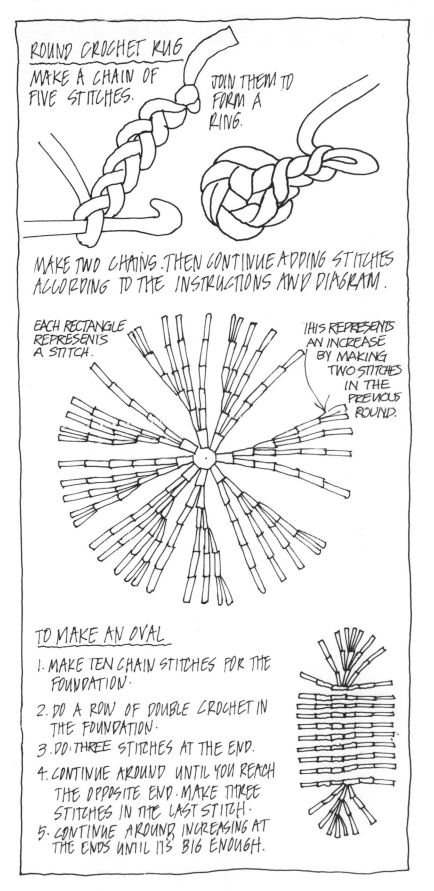

ROUND CROCHET RUG
MAKE A CHAIN OF FIVE STITCHES.

JOIN THEM TO FORM A RING.

MAKE TWO CHAINS. THEN CONTINUE ADDING STITCHES ACCORDING TO THE INSTRUCTIONS AND DIAGRAM.

EACH RECTANGLE REPRESENTS A STITCH.

THIS REPRESENTS AN INCREASE BY MAKING TWO STITCHES IN THE PREVIOUS ROUND.

TO MAKE AN OVAL

1. MAKE TEN CHAIN STITCHES FOR THE FOUNDATION.
2. DO A ROW OF DOUBLE CROCHET IN THE FOUNDATION.
3. DO THREE STITCHES AT THE END.
4. CONTINUE AROUND UNTIL YOU REACH THE OPPOSITE END. MAKE THREE STITCHES IN THE LAST STITCH.
5. CONTINUE AROUND INCREASING AT THE ENDS UNTIL IT'S BIG ENOUGH.

CHAIN STITCH

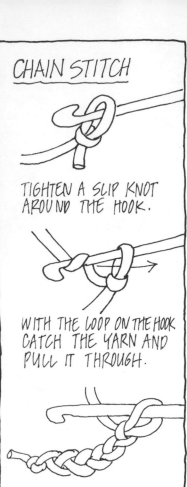

TIGHTEN A SLIP KNOT AROUND THE HOOK.

WITH THE LOOP ON THE HOOK CATCH THE YARN AND PULL IT THROUGH.

REPEAT TO MAKE A ROW OF CHAIN STITCHES.

MAKE A CIRCLE

MAKE A CHAIN OF 6 STITCHES. INSERT THE HOOK INTO THE LAST STITCH.

DRAW A LOOP THROUGH TO CLOSE THE CIRCLE.

SINGLE CROCHET

SECOND STITCH

FIRST

MAKE A CHAIN. INSERT THE HOOK INTO THE SECOND CHAIN.

WRAP THE YARN AROUND THE HOOK. PULL IT THROUGH.

YOU HAVE TWO LOOPS ON THE HOOK.

WRAP THE YARN AROUND THE HOOK. PULL IT THROUGH THE TWO LOOPS.

MAKE A STITCH IN EACH CHAIN.

March 20, 1978
La Grange, Indiana

Good morning:

Saw in the Quilters' Guide that you would like to have ideas how to use up old rags. So decided to send you the paper one of my weaver friends had printed. We have big looms and weave rugs out of old clothing. Although right now they have me quilting more than weaving, I like to do both. I feel you can save your left-over scraps for quilts and use up your old clothes by making them into rugs. I've woven many a rug out of old nylon stockings like it says in the paper. People like them . . .

Thank you,
Mrs. Henry L. Stutzman

We are of the Amish Faith. We are taught by our Parents not to waste anything. My birthdate is Dec. 25, 1911. Name Lydia.

Ragmen are a forgotten folk. Except for an occasional mention in literature and lore, few of us are likely to ever meet a ragman. It wasn't always so. Cities once had hundreds, even thousands, of them. Ragmen combed the countrysides and perused city alleys. Every house in the land was visited at least yearly by ragmen to see what rags of value might be had. Supplies of rags in quantity were necessary for the trade of a ragpicker to flourish. Consequently, it was not until fabrics were loomed in masses big enough to create leftovers and surpluses that the ragpicker's career began. Ragmen found a demand for their merchandise with the invention of the printing press.

Papermakers demanded vast quantities of rags. They used to beat the rags into a thick soup that was converted to paper for books, newspapers, and all manner of printed materials. Rag paper was the stock of all the printed word; and as the presses of Europe proliferated, the need for rags multiplied.

The life of a ragman was much like that of a peddler. Indeed some peddlers took rags for payment. In the cities, a ragman might push a cart. The more prosperous ragman might have a horse and travel appointed rounds through the countryside in the fashion of a peddler.

The life of the ragpicker in the cities was hardly romantic. Great ghettos of rag people grew on the outskirts of Paris and London and the other great cities. Bums, vagabonds, and beggarly folk could make a meager living by gathering the cities' refuse.

The tatters, as ragpickers were sometimes called, would bring their collections to a rag merchant. His warehouse could generally be found in a district outside the central part of the city. He would buy rags from anyone who collected them. Generally the horse-and-wagon collectors supplied the bulk of his trade, but people visited him throughout the day with small lots of rags. Street urchins traded a few rags for a penny or two in much the same way that kids today cash in bottles for nickels and dimes.

In the warehouse, the bales of rags were pulled apart and sorted by workers. Women were generally employed to cut off the buttons and rip off the seams. They were paid by the piece.

The most valuable rags were the white cotton and linen ones, which could be used by papermakers directly with little or no bleaching. Colored goods came next and would be used to make colored paper.

Later, machines were invented to pull apart wool and knitted rags. These were rewoven into a fabric called shoddy. We remember this in our language by calling all second-rate goods by this name. The remaining fiber was lumped together for flock or stuffing.

Folks who worked as rag sorters might set aside particularly handsome rags that came into their hands. At the day's end, they had the option of buying them to pass along to secondhand clothing dealers for a profit. This practice was a kind of bonus in an otherwise dirty and low-paying job.

The working conditions were grim. According to one description of a nineteenth-century rag merchant, the hours began at six-thirty in the morning and closing time was at six in the evening with half an hour for breakfast and forty-five minutes for lunch. A normal work week totaled sixty hours. To avoid the risk of fire, the buildings were unheated, so employees kept themselves warm by working faster or wrapping themselves in some of the rags.

CROCHETED BASKETS

These baskets look a lot like nests. In fact, they make good nests for your little treasures like jewelry or your precious pebble collection. You might even crochet a big chunky one to use as a breadbasket on the kitchen table. The method is very much like the one for the Crocheted Rug project. The only difference is that by skipping stitches, the work progresses in a bowl shape rather than being flat like a rug. They are quick, easy, and fun to have around. They are also fun to give away as a special gift wrap.

You can use T-shirt yarn, stretchy velour, or plain fabric strips to make this basket. Remember that fat yarn will make a chunkier, thicker-walled basket; while thinner yarn is best for a smaller, more finely crocheted basket. Try a few samples to get an idea of what you like.

You Will Need

At least a dozen yards of fabric strips for a small basket.
A large crochet hook. A number 7 will work well with average-sized T-shirt yarn. A larger wooden hook might be necessary with thicker rag yarn.

How to Do It

All baskets are made with a single crochet stitch or a half-double stitch worked in a circle. If you are not familiar with crochet terms, check the diagrams on page 80 or consult a basic crochet manual.
1. Form a circle with six chain stitches.
2. Make two more.
3. Commence with the single crochet stitch.
4. The work goes on in a circle, with each new row of stitches worked onto the last row. It's like building a pot with clay coils, only the coils are runs of crochet.

Rag Basket Crochet

To make the row smaller, skip every other or every third stitch. Skipping to every third stitch will make it very small, very quickly.

To make a row larger, increase its size by doing two stitches in one hole or two stitches in every other hole.

You can stretch and pull the fabric with your fingers to give it shape as you go.

CROCHET A ROUND BASE. USE THE RAG RUG INSTRUCTIONS.

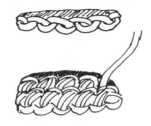

BASE: SIDE VIEW

AFTER YOU MAKE THE BASE CONTINUE CROCHETING TO BUILD UP THE WALLS.

TO MAKE THE WALLS WIDER, INCREASE.

TO INCREASE

DO TWO STITCH-ES IN THE SAME FOUN-DATION STITCH.

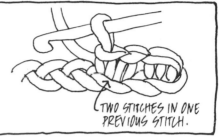

TWO STITCHES IN ONE PREVIOUS STITCH.

TO MAKE THE WALLS NARROWER, DECREASE.

TO DECREASE

SKIP A STITCH IN THE FOUN-DATION.

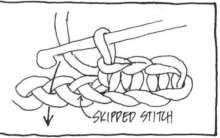

SKIPPED STITCH

YOU CAN INCREASE OR DECREASE EACH STITCH OR EVERY SECOND OR THIRD STITCH ACCORDING TO HOW QUICKLY YOU WANT TO WIDEN OR NARROW THE BASKET CONTOUR. EXPERIMENT.

MANY SHAPES AND TEXTURES ARE POSSIBLE.

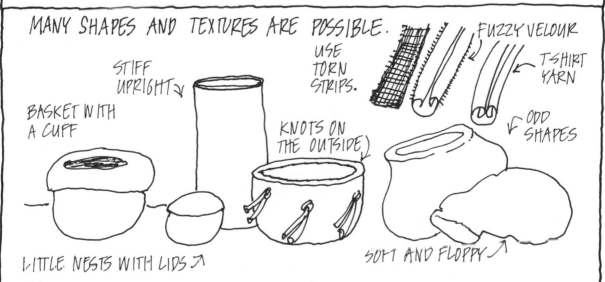

STIFF UPRIGHT↓

USE TORN STRIPS.

FUZZY VELOUR

T-SHIRT YARN

BASKET WITH A CUFF

KNOTS ON THE OUTSIDE

ODD SHAPES

LITTLE NESTS WITH LIDS↗

SOFT AND FLOPPY↗

BOUND BASKETS

People have been tying things together for thousands of years—probably ever since some primitive soul in a far-off time discovered that by carrying things strung together, a person could carry a lot more things. Since then humans have been collecting and adding to and improving their knowledge of how to bind things together.

Basketmaking is a craft of binding together that has reached an evolved state. Anthropologists believe that the craft of basketmaking led to the invention of woven cloth.

Indians of the Americas in the last century wove this legacy into amazing articles for ceremony and everyday use. Their beautiful baskets held water, cooked food, and cradled babies. Their intricate designs even told stories.

These days, fiber artists and plain folk alike are taking an interest in making and collecting baskets. Rag baskets are a colorful new way to practice this ancient art.

This method of making bound baskets has been used in many parts of the world. The technique works well using T-shirt yarn and clothesline rope instead of the more traditional reeds and raffias.

You Will Need

A package of clothesline rope.
At least 10 to 15 yards of T-shirt yarn.
A needle and thread.

How to Do It

1. Cut the end of the rope to a point.
2. Wrap the yarn around the rope. Do it so that the raw edges are turned toward the inside. Wrap so that each wrap overlaps the last one.

3. When it is long enough, coil the rope into a circle and secure it as shown.
4. Continue wrapping. At every third wrap, catch two thicknesses of rope. Continue in this way until you have a coil the size you want for the base. To shape the basket, wrap the rope, then give it a tug to pull the walls up. Shape it as you go along.

Keep building until you have a shape you like.
5. To finish, cut off the rope at an angle and wrap down to the end. Stitch with needle and thread.

> "Willful waste makes woeful want."
>
> James Kelly,
> Scottish Proverbs, 1739

TO WRAP COILS

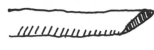

A. CUT THE END OF THE ROPE TO A POINT.

B. WRAP THE ROPE WITH THE BINDING.

TURN THE RAW EDGES INSIDE. LET THE WRAPPING TOUCH.

TO COIL THE BASKET

C. CURVE THE TIP. PULL IT INTO PLACE WITH A FIGURE 8 WRAP.

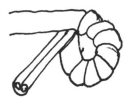

D. TUCK THE TIP IN. WRAP IT TO THE NEXT COIL.

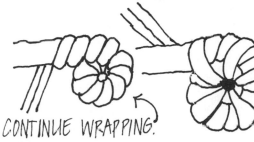

JOIN A NEW YARN BY TUCKING THE OLD END UNDER A NEW WRAP.

CONTINUE WRAPPING.

EVERY THIRD WRAP CATCH TWO THICKNESSES OF ROPE. CONTINUE UNTIL THE COIL IS BIG ENOUGH FOR THE BASE.

BUILD UP THE WALLS WITH LAYERS OF ROPE.

GIVE THE ROPE A TUG TO PULL THE WALLS UP.

KEEP BUILDING UNTIL YOU HAVE A SHAPE YOU LIKE.

MAKE A SLIGHTLY LARGER BOWL FOR A LID.

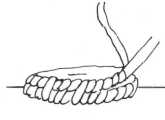

MANY SHAPES ARE POSSIBLE.

TO FINISH, CUT THE ROPE TO A POINT. BIND IT ALONG THE EDGE. TUCK IN THE END.

October 25, 1977

Dear Linda Allison,

I first started using rags in coiled baskets — rags that came from friends who were often reluctant to give them up. Something that's because a rag has been loved a lot. I always asked "the story" behind the rag. For instance, one beach towel, wonderfully old and faded, belonged to friends of mine while they were courting many years ago. I made a basket for them from it.

Lately, I've been working on old baby quilts; which are all but rags — I love them ragged and falling apart.

Marilyn Green
Palo Alto, CA

P.S. I bet you can find a version of "Cinderella" with mention of rags. Also "The Little Match Girl." Seems like they always describe them as "dressed in rags."

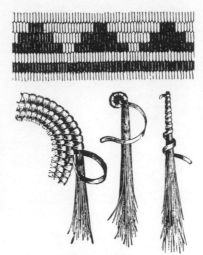

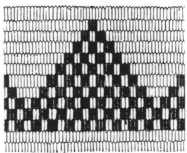

Indian basketmakers created some pretty amazing results in pattern and scale using the coil binding technique and natural materials. Perhaps you can do the same using rags.

Flour-Sack Fiasco

My mother used to make clothes out of old clothes. She made me a coat out of hand-me-down old coats. She made all my clothes, because we couldn't buy them. Mama also made my underwear out of flour sacks. They were bloomers, not bikinis like you wear today. They had a little elastic on the legs and a little elastic around the waist. They used some kind of grease and soap that they'd put on the flour sack, and they'd lather it up and roll it up and leave it over-night. That was supposed to take the writing off the flour sacks. And I guess that Mama made them a little too big or something, and she didn't quite get all the marking off the back side of the pants.

There was one boy at school. He was really mean. He would get me in tears. He wasn't teasing just because he wanted to play. He was just mean. He used to tease me about my mother being a Mexican, how she talked with her arms. Oh dear, Mama used to go and call him an s.o.b. everytime he turned around. She was really fiery. She'd say you little s.o.b., don't you tease my daughter. It wouldn't do a bit of good 'cause then he would tease me all the more.

Anyway she didn't get it all off. My dress must have been short or something. And I guess I must 'a' been playing, and then I bent over and he saw that, oh God, all he had to do was to see that. I never wore those pants to school again. He liked to tease me to death about my "Sperry pants."

Interview with Mary Ivie,
July 1978

FUROSHIKI

"The *furoshiki* is a substitute for how we would use the paper bag when we go to the store, like a department store, and buy something. Traditionally when you go to the store you bring your own *furoshiki* and say, 'I'll wrap it in this' or 'would you please wrap it in this.' People can carry the day's shopping in it. Kids and workmen too carry their lunches in a *furoshiki*. They have a lunch box inside.

"They are always square and pretty good sized (about 18 or 20 inches square). A lot of times they are silk. Usually they are purple or magenta. Those are the most common. The ones I have are cotton, blue and white. These are more folk craftsy, not so common.

"When we were working on the construction site, the maid from the house would bring down a snack to us at three, and it would be a tray of candy or cookies or something and a pot full of tea. She would carry the pot in one hand and the tray with cookies and cups she would wrap in the *furoshiki*. She'd be able to carry it all at once with the help of the *furoshiki;* otherwise she would have had to carry it in a basket.

"I was studying Kendo, Japanese fencing with the bamboo sword. I had to get my mask fixed. And when I went to pick it up, they were going to put in in a paper bag. When I said, 'No, wait a minute, wrap it in this [a *furoshiki*],' they were surprised."

Interview with Stephen
Freidland, January 1978

You Will Need

An 18- or 20-inch square of sturdy fabric. A washable variety is best.

How to Do It

1. Hem the edges of the square with a 1/4-inch hem all the way around. Machine stitching is fine.
2. To use the *furoshiki* as a carrier, place whatever you want to carry in the center of the cloth.
3. Bring two diagonal corners together to the center and tie them securely with a square knot.
4. Do the same for the other two corners.
5. Carry the *furoshiki* by slipping your hand under the folds.

A *furoshiki* can hold all sorts of loose things. It also makes a great wrapping for a box. In fact the traditional Japanese lunch pail is wrapped in just such a cloth.

Old Clothes,
Any Old Clo', Clo'

If I'd as much money
As I could tell,
I never would cry,
Old clothes to sell!
Old clothes to sell!
Old clothes to sell!
I never would cry,
Old clothes to sell!

A traditional rhyme

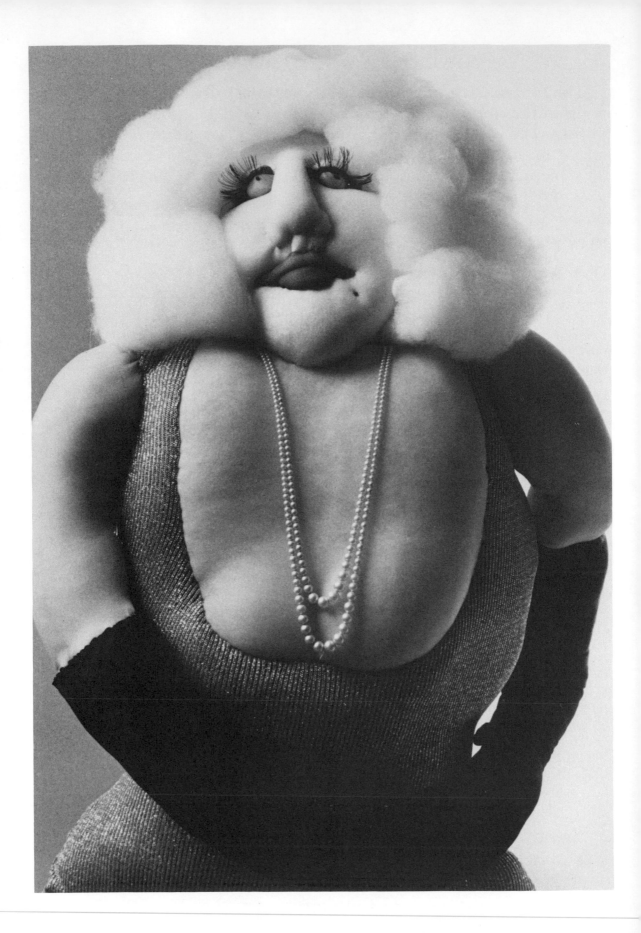

4

Rag People

CLOTH DOLLS have probably been around almost as long as cloth. Dolls have been found in Egyptian and Greek tombs and still survive today in this age of supertechnology. Perhaps this is because they seem to become more than the sum of their humble materials, taking on uncanny personas— often not at all what their makers intended. It is this quality that makes it easy to believe that dolls have lives and spirits all their own. We may relegate them to the nursery as the playthings of children, but they have often been used for more serious purposes: influencing the harvest, the weather, the health of friends—and enemies. In some cultures, to create and manipulate a doll was to possess power over life itself.

We still use dolls in primitive and superstitious ways. We make life-sized effigies, called scarecrows, in our own image to guard our gardens. Certainly every serious gardener knows that the birds only laugh at them. Perhaps they are remnants from a ritual of the harvest spirit. Even in these enlightened times, unpopular persons are created in cloth and tortured in effigy. Burning such an effigy is still a powerful statement — powerful enough in some parts of the world to get a person into serious political trouble.

Today, in the age of space science and sophisticated technology, dolls are still very much a part of our lives. Think of the superhero dolls, who embody qualities of strength and immortality in their bionic parts, or their female counterparts, with eternally young bodies of goddesslike dimensions and hair that can be styled. These dolls seem not so much to be playthings as they are examples of how we think people in our society ought to be, or how we wish we were.

And of course children and other persons of candor still confide in their dolls. You, yourself, may remember having consulted with your favorite doll or teddy bear on matters of great importance. Maybe you still have that special old bear. It is not so unusual to find a grown-up person who still keeps track of a tattered and worn teddy. In these days of our use-it-and-throw-it-away lifestyle, it must be that these cloth creatures truly have a special power over us.

STOCKING DOLLS

Sophisticated cousins of the old-fashioned sock doll, these creatures are more like soft sculpture. Made from stockings, they have a fat, fleshy feel. And a few stitches with a needle turns a stuffed sock into a personality, with a face that can be silly, sad, or — as a friend put it — "downright scary."

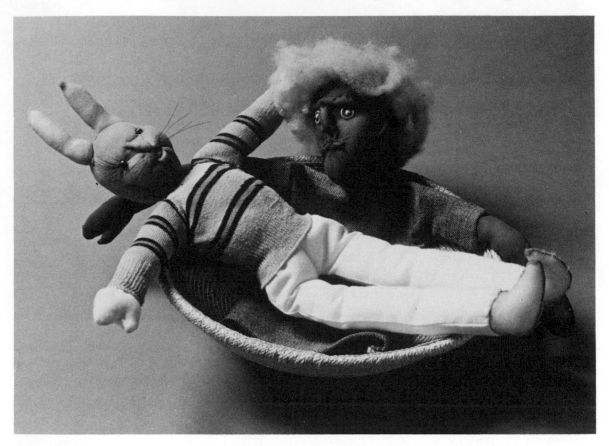

You Will Need

One heavy nylon stocking or a pair of tights.
Some dacron stuffing.
Needle and thread.
Buttons or beads for eyes.

Basic Body

1. Cut the body, arms, and legs from a single stocking.
2. To make the body, bind one end of the body section. Stuff the head with a piece of batting the size of a tennis ball. (Now is a good time to work on the features.)

3. Bind the head where you want the chin to be. Stick in a pencil stub to stiffen it.
4. Stitch around the arms and legs with a 1/4-inch seam allowance, leaving the ends open.
5. Stuff.
6. Stuff the torso.
7. Stitch on the arms and legs.

Giving It Shape

8. Here comes the fun part. You can shape the body by molding it with your hands. Add a few running stitches for creases. Add a few stitches for dimples and bellybuttons. (Flex the knees and stitch in the toes.)

To Form the Features

9. Basically, to build up a bulge, add more stuffing. If you want a line, put in a row of running stitches. For creases pull the stitches tight.

> *"Rags are royal raiment when worn for virtue's sake."*
>
> *Franklin,*
> Poor Richard's Almanac,
> *1735*

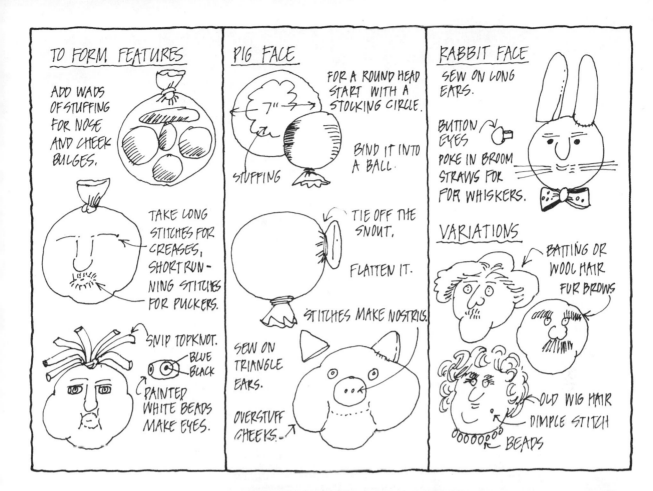

TO FORM FEATURES

ADD WADS OF STUFFING FOR NOSE AND CHEEK BULGES.

TAKE LONG STITCHES FOR CREASES, SHORT RUNNING STITCHES FOR PUCKERS.

SNIP TOPKNOT. BLUE BLACK PAINTED WHITE BEADS MAKE EYES.

PIG FACE

FOR A ROUND HEAD START WITH A STOCKING CIRCLE.

STUFFING

BIND IT INTO A BALL.

TIE OFF THE SNOUT.

FLATTEN IT.

STITCHES MAKE NOSTRILS.

SEW ON TRIANGLE EARS.

OVERSTUFF CHEEKS.

RABBIT FACE

SEW ON LONG EARS.

BUTTON EYES
POKE IN BROOM STRAWS FOR FOR WHISKERS.

VARIATIONS

BATTING OR WOOL HAIR FUR BROWS

OLD WIG HAIR
DIMPLE STITCH
BEADS

Stocking Lore

The first stockings were cut from cloth. Not until knitting was invented in the fifteenth century did stockings with stretch appear. They were a runaway success. A large number of English persons made their living knitting stockings. So many did this that Queen Elizabeth refused to grant a patent on a knitting machine for fear it might jeopardize the livelihood of many of her subjects. She did concede that she might consider such an invention if it could make the silk stockings of which she was so fond.

This illustration (right) shows an old stockinger and his wife, who for many years worked together on hand stocking frames.

91

Hoo-Doo Doll

. . . the conjurer who was making the charm named it "Charley Leland," and talked to it, having it answer him back by ventriloquism. Their directions were that the ball should be wrapped in tinfoil and a little silk rag, and then be slung under the right armpit in a linen bag. It must be taken out once a week and bathed in whiskey to keep its strength from dying. At any time "He" could be taken out and consulted or be confided in and his approval or disapproval could be felt by the owner. The author says, "The hoo-doo doctors of my acquaintance recommend the 'tricks' to be doused well with whiskey to bring them to their full power. . . ."

Newbell Niles Puckett,
*Folk Beliefs of the
Southern Negro*

Stocking finishing machine (1927).

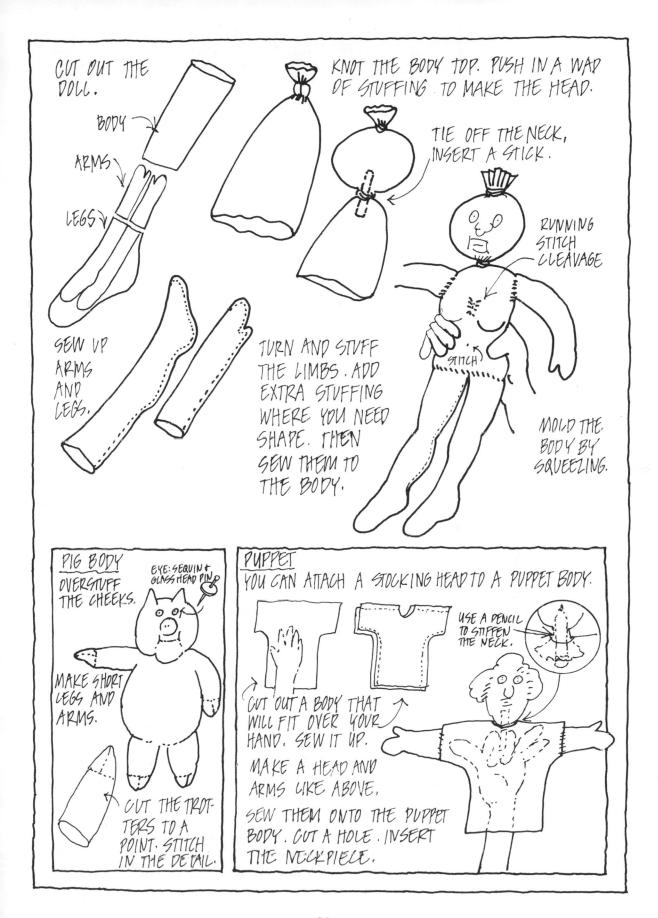

CUT OUT THE DOLL.

BODY

ARMS

LEGS

KNOT THE BODY TOP. PUSH IN A WAD OF STUFFING TO MAKE THE HEAD.

TIE OFF THE NECK, INSERT A STICK.

RUNNING STITCH CLEAVAGE

STITCH

SEW UP ARMS AND LEGS.

TURN AND STUFF THE LIMBS. ADD EXTRA STUFFING WHERE YOU NEED SHAPE. THEN SEW THEM TO THE BODY.

MOLD THE BODY BY SQUEEZING.

PIG BODY
OVERSTUFF THE CHEEKS.

EYE: SEQUIN + GLASS HEAD PIN

MAKE SHORT LEGS AND ARMS.

CUT THE TROT-TERS TO A POINT. STITCH IN THE DETAIL.

PUPPET
YOU CAN ATTACH A STOCKING HEAD TO A PUPPET BODY.

USE A PENCIL TO STIFFEN THE NECK.

CUT OUT A BODY THAT WILL FIT OVER YOUR HAND. SEW IT UP.

MAKE A HEAD AND ARMS LIKE ABOVE.

SEW THEM ONTO THE PUPPET BODY. CUT A HOLE. INSERT THE NECKPIECE.

POLITICAL RAGS

At the end of October, in England, children begin to appear on the street in the company of weird-looking fellows. By the beginning of November, you are likely to see children and their lumpy dummies on any street corner. These children solicit passers-by with the question, "Penny for the Guy?" If you are unfamiliar with this phenomenon, you have no idea what to answer or whether you should answer at all. You begin to wonder whether or not this might be a fund raiser for the deformed or perhaps some sort of campaign by cuckoo children.

Neither is the case; however the real reason behind these goings on is just as unlikely. These perfectly normal children are parading these bizarre effigies to do what children love to do best — collect money to squander on fireworks and sweets. This odd custom is perpetrated in honor of Guy Fawkes, whose day is celebrated by a national frenzy of effigy making and money raising. Children all over England spend hours of their spare time stuffing cast-off clothing. The results are some rather ungainly humanoids who often have torsoes and legs of completely unmatched proportions. Guys are usually placed on some sort of wheeled vehicle for an easy trip to the local street corner. There they sit in slumped splendor, silent partners in the solicitations for fireworks money. Guys lead short, colorful lives. The fate of these poor stuffed persons is to be torched on Bonfire Night with the other local Guys, accompanied by shows of fireworks and general high spirits.

All of these effigies are made in memory of one Guy Fawkes, who was a member of a ring of conspirators plotting against the crown to blow up Parliament. In those days, Catholics were making their discontent known to their English overlords. This particular group of discontents had taken their grievances underground. Guy and his band had the cellars underneath Parliament stocked with a large amount of gunpowder. It was to be exploded as the king walked into the chambers on the following day. Everything was in place when the plot was discovered on the eve of November 4. The plotters were rounded up and executed in a painful fashion in the year of 1606. It seems that once was not enough for poor old Guy. He is executed in effigy thousands of times again each November 4.

GUYS

There seems to be no reason why the delight of making a Guy should be restricted to those who know about Charles the First and his brush with the Gunpowder Plotters. These large, lumpy fellows are fun to make and fit right into our equivalent holiday of sweets and merrymaking — Halloween. In fact, both holidays are probably the remains of an older festival that was celebrated with bonfires in remembrance of departed spirits. In any case, a couple of Guys on your front porch will lend a bit of life to your Halloween decorations.

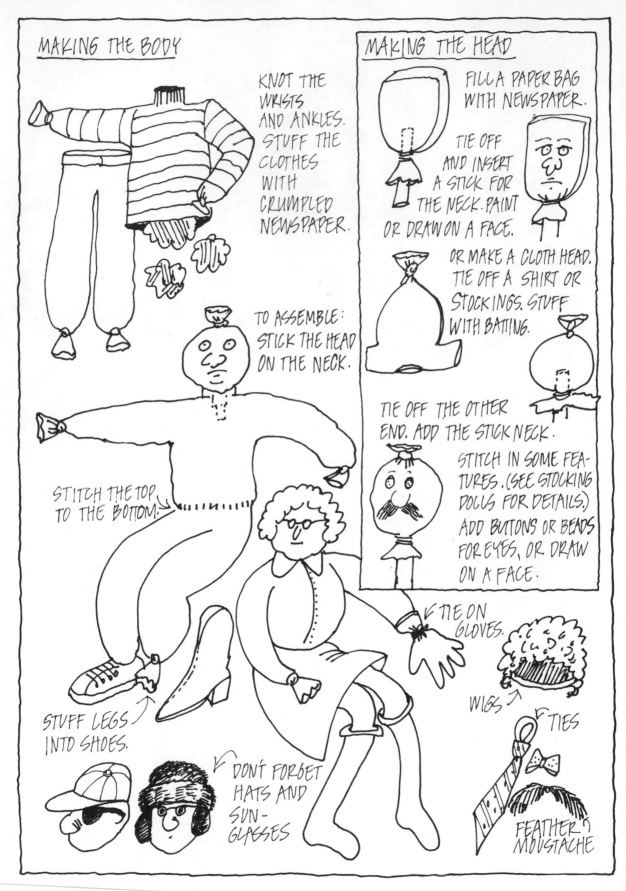

MAKING THE BODY

KNOT THE WRISTS AND ANKLES. STUFF THE CLOTHES WITH CRUMPLED NEWSPAPER.

TO ASSEMBLE: STICK THE HEAD ON THE NECK.

STITCH THE TOP TO THE BOTTOM.

STUFF LEGS INTO SHOES.

DON'T FORGET HATS AND SUN-GLASSES

MAKING THE HEAD

FILL A PAPER BAG WITH NEWSPAPER.

TIE OFF AND INSERT A STICK FOR THE NECK. PAINT OR DRAW ON A FACE.

OR MAKE A CLOTH HEAD. TIE OFF A SHIRT OR STOCKINGS. STUFF WITH BATTING.

TIE OFF THE OTHER END. ADD THE STICK NECK.

STITCH IN SOME FEATURES. (SEE STOCKING DOLLS FOR DETAILS.) ADD BUTTONS OR BEADS FOR EYES, OR DRAW ON A FACE.

TIE ON GLOVES.

WIGS

TIES

FEATHER MOUSTACHE

96

You Will Need

Old clothes: long-sleeved shirt and long pants are required. Hats, shoes, gloves, and socks will add character. Wigs, sunglasses, everything should be related in size. A kid's shirt and outsized pants won't work.

A pile of newspaper for stuffing.

A paper bag or a length of double knit for the head.

Markers or paint for drawing on the face.

How to Do It

1. Knot the bottoms of the pants and the wrists of the shirt. Button and zip all the fastenings closed.
2. Wad up the newspaper and stuff it into the pants and the shirt. Stuff them until they are full and they begin to take the shape you want.
3. Sew the shirt to the trousers.
4. Make the head by stuffing a paper bag or a piece of knit. Gather up the loose ends and insert a length of stick into the head for the neck. Tie the ends around the stick with a piece of string. Draw the features on.
5. Fasten the head to the body.
6. Add on socks, shoes, gloves, a hat — whatever you turn up from the old clothes pile that seems right.
7. Draw on a face. You can sculpt out a nose by taking stitches in appropriate spots.
8. Set up your Guy.

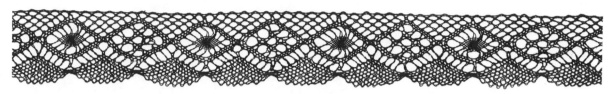

RAG FANTASIES

Marilyn Green is a connoisseur of rags. She uses them in her stitcheries and in the workshops and classes she teaches. She is especially intrigued by the many stories that they suggest and the histories hidden behind their surfaces. She is a collector of rag portraits — pictures of rags taken from real life: things such as a kite tail abandoned in a tree, rags decorating a scarecrow in a garden, scraps of cloth found in mud flats, and strips of cloth flying as a warning from a fence. But to tell it in her words:

". . . the first thing that comes to mind concerning why I like rags is the wonderful subtle, faded colors they take on as the fabric fades and gets worn. It's similar to what happens to copper when it's left out to take on that wonderful green color or, I suppose, to people as they age and get grey hair (or it falls out — which also happens to threads in rags — I guess that's called stretching the metaphor). When I am actually using rags in my work, these faded colors are very important to the art, as I like to work with the idea of a landscape that is mysterious. A person looking at it decides whether it is the land, sea, or sky. I find that the subtle colors work very well for me here.

"I once wrote an article about abandoned shoes — the single shoe that everyone sees along the roadside or way off by itself in the wilderness. The pictures I take of rags are similar. I try to imagine what the rag once was, if I can't tell from its shape. If it evolved out of being a piece of clothing. This imagining is very romantic. I make up stories about what the cloth once was and where it might have been in its life.

It's hard to define how I use them for inspiration. I guess I like the idea that they look so ephemeral — when indeed they are *very* durable creatures who have been around a long while. They're good jumping-off points for fantasies. I sometimes teach classes in design, and I will compose slide shows which show fabric used in many different ways. The slides of rags really show fabric in its most beautiful, flowing way."

STUFFED LADIES

These persons are a kind of soft sculpture drawn in two dimensions, then stuffed to give them form. Use bits of lace and trim from your scrap bag to decorate them and give them texture. Make a couple or a whole family related in form, color, and texture.

You Will Need

Black cotton thread.
Tissue paper.
Scraps of white or flesh-colored cotton.
Polyester batting.
Trim scraps.
Print or solid cotton scraps.

To Make the Face

1. Make a drawing of a face on a sheet of tissue paper. Copy the one in this book or make your own.
2. Pin the tissue-paper face to a piece of white or flesh-colored cotton fabric.
3. Thread your sewing machine with black cotton thread.
4. You are now ready to stitch up a face. Do this by sewing along and right through the tissue paper lines onto the fabric. Use medium-sized stitches. Experiment and have a good time stitching forward and backward and changing the stitch sizes when it feels right. Expect to get a bit off the track here and there. That is what gives these faces their wonderful individuality.

To Make the Body

1. Cut a front and back from contrasting fabrics. Prints are good.
2. Stitch on the head, front and back, to each body, front and back. This curved seam is easier to handle with hand stitching. Clip.

3. Choose a trim according to your whim and the contents of your scrap bag. Ribbons, bits of lace or braid, buttons and beads all are possibilities. The best way to approach this is to rummage out everything possible from your trim scraps until you get a combination you like. Machine stitch the trim to the front and the back or decorate just the front.
4. Right sides together, stitch the doll together leaving a section open so you can stuff it.

5. Clip, turn, and stuff the body.
6. Construct the arms by cutting them from fabric to match the face. Stitch and stuff.
7. Open up the sleeves. Insert the arms and stitch them onto the body by hand.

EACH SQUARE EQUALS 2"

CUT A PAPER PATTERN FOR THE BODY AND THE HEAD AND ARMS. USE THE DIAGRAM AND ENLARGE IT SO IT IS 20" HIGH.

CUT OUT THE BODY FRONT AND BACK. USE ONE FABRIC OR SEVERAL KINDS.

CUT THESE FROM PINK OR TAN FABRIC.

8"

10"

2"

TO MAKE THE FACE

TRACE THE PATTERN ONTO PAPER.

DRAW IN THE FEATURES.

EMBROIDER IT WITH A SEWING MACHINE (SEE INSTRUCTIONS).

CUT IT OUT.

VARIATIONS AND TRIM

BEADS

FEATHERS

STRAIGHT NECK

LACE

APPLIQUE

RIBBONS

BUTTONS

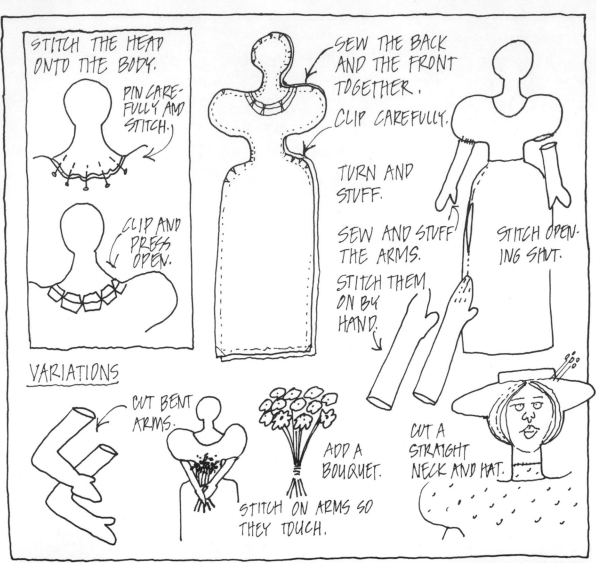

STITCH THE HEAD ONTO THE BODY.

PIN CAREFULLY AND STITCH.

CLIP AND PRESS OPEN.

SEW THE BACK AND THE FRONT TOGETHER.

CLIP CAREFULLY.

TURN AND STUFF.

SEW AND STUFF THE ARMS.

STITCH THEM ON BY HAND.

STITCH OPENING SHUT.

VARIATIONS

CUT BENT ARMS.

ADD A BOUQUET.

STITCH ON ARMS SO THEY TOUCH.

CUT A STRAIGHT NECK AND HAT.

Lost Looks

Sometimes a rag person would wear to such a deplorable state that a whole new replacement would make more sense. But who can be sensible about somebody they love? So when the cheeks paled or when the lips lost their luster, it was often the custom for rag dolls to get touchups or sometimes a whole new face sewn on top of the old one. Dolls have been discovered with layers of old faces. If you could bear to perform surgery on an antique rag person who is worn with love, you might find that it has worn a number of faces.

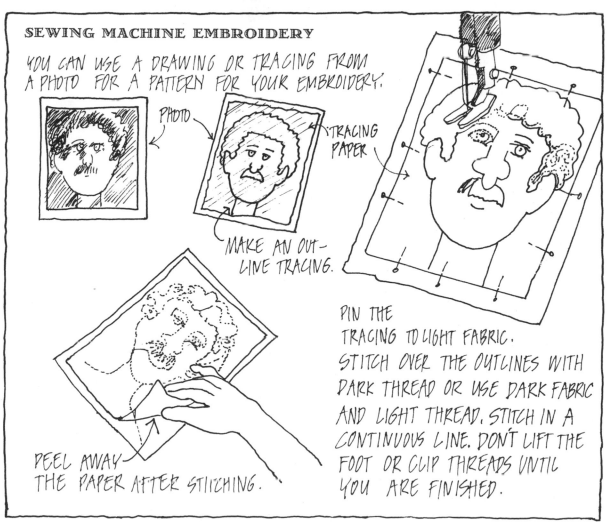

SEWING MACHINE EMBROIDERY

YOU CAN USE A DRAWING OR TRACING FROM A PHOTO FOR A PATTERN FOR YOUR EMBROIDERY.

PHOTO

TRACING PAPER

MAKE AN OUTLINE TRACING.

PEEL AWAY THE PAPER AFTER STITCHING.

PIN THE TRACING TO LIGHT FABRIC. STITCH OVER THE OUTLINES WITH DARK THREAD OR USE DARK FABRIC AND LIGHT THREAD. STITCH IN A CONTINUOUS LINE. DON'T LIFT THE FOOT OR CLIP THREADS UNTIL YOU ARE FINISHED.

GIVE YOUR DOLL A HEART

A BUTTON.

A BAUBLE FROM YOUR JEWELRY BOX.

CARVE ONE FROM WOOD.

CUT ONE FROM FELT. SEW IT ONTO THE BODY.

SEW THE ABOVE HEARTS INTO THE BODY.

PAINT A HEART DIRECTLY ONTO THE DOLL'S CHEST.

STITCH IN FINGER DETAILS.

GIVE YOUR DOLL A HISTORY

WRITE YOUR DOLL'S HISTORY ONTO A COTTON OR RIBBON TAG. USE INDELIBLE LAUNDRY MARKER WITH A FINE POINT. SEW THE TAG INTO A SEAM OR DIRECTLY ONTO THE DOLL.

Emma ragdoll was made for Sarah by Grandma Violet on her birthday 1978

THE TRUE STORY OF RAGGEDY ANN

Raggedy Ann is a very familiar face to most folks today. So familiar that it's hard for us to think of a time when children have not played with this lovable stuffed lady with the gentle smile.

The truth is that Raggedy Ann was born in an attic in Indianapolis in 1917. It is probably more correct to say reborn, because Raggedy Ann had already lived in this particular attic for some years in a barrel with only some odds and ends for company. Her rediscoverer, a gentleman called Johnny Gruelle, was a resident of the house attached to the particular attic. Gruelle was an illustrator for a local newspaper. As it happened, one afternoon he was rummaging around in the attic for something or other when he came across her smiling face at the bottom of a barrel. Undaunted by her crumpled posture and faded looks, he lifted her from her barrel retreat and carried her downstairs.

Curious about this rag lady's past, he conferred with his mother, who happened to be visiting him at the time. It turned out that she and the doll were childhood friends. The doll had been made for her when she was a small girl. She had been a cherished companion, even though time had relegated her to the attic. Of course, after the years of hard knocks and hugs, the rag doll had lost a bit of her sparkle and shine; but what she'd lost in looks, she'd gained in character. Something in her faded face appealed to the artist in Gruelle. He got out his paints and retouched her lips and lashes. He christened her Raggedy Ann. Her charm quickly made her the favorite of Gruelle's daughter, Marcella.

Not many weeks later, Gruelle wrote and illustrated a story starring Raggedy Ann. Within a few months, the book was sold and published. This was the beginning of fame and fortune for the red-headed rag doll. Story followed story until twenty-six of them were in print describing Raggedy Ann's adventures with her friend, Raggedy Andy.

Her founder died in 1938, but Raggedy Ann lives on. Every year thousands of copies of her adventures are sold. She has appeared in films and comic strips. She has decorated clocks, sheets, and electric toothbrushes. And every night millions of her copyrighted descendants are taken to bed and are literally loved to destruction.

As I talk, I can sort of see him, exactly where he was and what he looked like. It's amazing. Ragmen were interesting figures. They had an element of mystery about them. It's like out of the fog. They came with a nice regularity — you knew that there were constants in life. And the fact that there were constants in life. And the fact that one's universe in these kinds of neighborhoods (in Brooklyn in the 1930s and 1940s) was limited to a few blocks. This ragman came from the outer world, not that he led a very romantic life — but I remember he had a very appealing, kind, grandfatherly face. He was a very soft-spoken, kindly sort. You always had the feeling that he had failed his Ph. D. qualifying exams in Poland and that now he was reduced to collecting *schmatas*.

I don't think that I have ever seen one younger than fifty or fifty-five and invariably no taller than five feet two. Maybe they were originally taller but with the weight of carrying around those rags . . . They were typically dressed in beat-up clothes, as if their clothes were no better than the clothes that they were collecting. They probably were the same — typically with a black cap. One really got the feeling that they wore the same clothes in Poland that they did here. Always black.

He would come down the street and yell, *"schmatas, schmatas."* Or I seem to remember that occasionally he would yell, *"old clothes."* *Schmata* means essentially rag in Yiddish. I think that later on as things became more Americanized he would even call out in English. There would sometimes be conversations and they would invariably be in Yiddish. So I assume that they were always Jewish.

He would walk down the alleys between the apartment buildings and yell out. The word would often precede him by a few houses. The reason that it would go ahead is not because this was a great occasion for celebration, but because it would allow housewives to gather up the old clothes that were in the back of the closet.

Generally the apartments were small. There were three or four kids living in them, and they would have very few closets. Remember the old Fibber McGee closets? Well, that's exactly the way these closets were. It was imperative that you throw your old stuff out.

But the idea of putting clothes in the garbage can simply did not exist. I remember my mother saying the *schmata* man will be around next week, so keep it. It was like the food business we grow up with, the eat-there-are-starving-kids-in-China type thing. It was very much the same thing with clothes. There were poor kids somewhere, and somehow there was something inherently evil in throwing away something that was still useful.

So when he came, people would dig into their closets and pull out some type of bundle. You could in fact hear him when he was a few houses away, and somehow there was a very effective grapevine so that everyone knew that he was on his way. I can remember an aunt calling up my mother saying, "Esther, the *schmata* man is working his way up the street." You would generally open up the window and shout down, "I have some stuff for you." You would either throw it down or if it was a big bundle, he would say, "I'm coming up." It would take him about fifteen minutes to climb the stairs. There were no elevators in those buildings. He would be dragging his black sack, the equivalent of a huge laundry bag. He'd knock on the door and be very polite and perhaps chat for a few minutes. Always the same person. In fact, I can remember only one.

They stopped coming in later years. I don't know why, perhaps affluence. I don't remember them past my early teens [around 1945]. It could have been a case of passing on. It was hardly the type of thing that you would train your son to be. They were all typically immigrants, and they came at a time when people tended to be untrained.

It was amazing. You know they were older, but they walked long distances. I don't know how they did it in fact. He didn't live in the immediate neighborhood. He was simply this figure who would materialize out of the mist somehow. I don't think anyone knew him personally. He was mysterious. He had one sole function in life and that was to collect *schmatas*. Then he would disappear. For the next month he was out of your life; then the next month, he would come again.

Interview with Stan Berger,
August 1978

5

Rags to Give

OUTSIDE THE WINDOW rain drifted down from the gray sky. Sitting there, elbows propped on the sill, she felt dismal and dull, as if one of those clouds were stuck inside of her. The month was December.

Still looking out, her eye was caught by a bobbing yellow figure. She recognized her small friend, Peter. A smile lit her face as she watched him slop through puddles in his galoshes and mackintosh.

Peter, at three years, was full of wonder and these days his wonderful thoughts were on Christmas. She delighted in listening to his chatter. As his bright eyes grew large, he talked about his favorite things: ponies. More than anything he wanted a pony.

Hearing his wishes, she imagined being his fairy godmother. She would grant him each and every wish with the true benevolence characteristic of fairy godmothers, asking for nothing more than to witness his joy.

The only problem was that she lacked a magic wand. She had hardly any money to spare for such purposes, but she was determined and so she schemed. Finally she had an idea.

Pulling on her raincoat, she bounded down the stairs and out the door. She knew where she was going. Uphill to catch the Number 85. Off at the seventh stop. Half a block's walk. She pushed through the door of the Salvation Army store. Past the machine full of faded gumballs. Past old ladies parked in musty overstuffed chairs. Down a narrow aisle through swollen racks of old clothes. At the aisle's end she stopped. There under a bare light bulb was a jumble of rags. She dug into the heap, laying aside an occasional piece of cloth.

It took a while to find the right pieces, but she did. When they were paid for and packaged, she tucked them under her arm and left. Outside the rain was still coming down. She didn't notice as she headed home.

She was totally absorbed in her work the rest of that day while she bent in concentration over the small table. Her light burned well into the night, and the steady rhythm of her sewing machine could be heard. She did seem to be working some kind of magic.

Then she was finished. Amid the scraps on the table rested a pony, Peter's pony, from the shining button eyes to the tip of its broom-handle tail. On its face it wore a silly grin that must have been contagious, because, as she turned off the light and stood in the dark looking out the window, she too wore a smile.

107

RIBBON BASKETS

Ribbon baskets make colorful catchers for your little treasures. In bright-colored satin or grosgrain ribbon, they are something of a treasure in themselves. You will need a number of lengths of ribbon that are of equal widths. If your scrap bag is lacking in the ribbon department, pay a visit to your local fabric store. The larger ones often have scrap bags of ribbon remnants. The mill ends from a factory are a real deal, if you don't mind potluck colors.

You Will Need

For a basket 3 inches deep and 2 1/2 inches wide:
Eight pieces of 3/4-inch wide grosgrain ribbon, each 14 inches long.
Or for a basket 2 1/2 inches deep and 3 1/2 inches wide:
Twelve pieces of 1/2-inch wide satin ribbon, each 14 inches long.
Some cellophane tape.
A needle and thread.

How to Do It

1. Start with an even number of strands at right angles to one another. Weave them into place.
2. Baste or fasten them so that all the edges touch.
3. When you begin to weave the sides, fold and press the base in the manner shown.
4. When the base is pressed, the strips will naturally cross each other on a diagonal.

Continue to weave the sides in an over-under fashion, pulling them taut around the corners. (Hold them in place with tape.)

There are two ways to finish the edges. Baste around upper edge. Trim and bind the raw edge with a piece of ribbon. Or fold to inside on the diagonal and tuck the ends back over themselves. Weave them into the body.

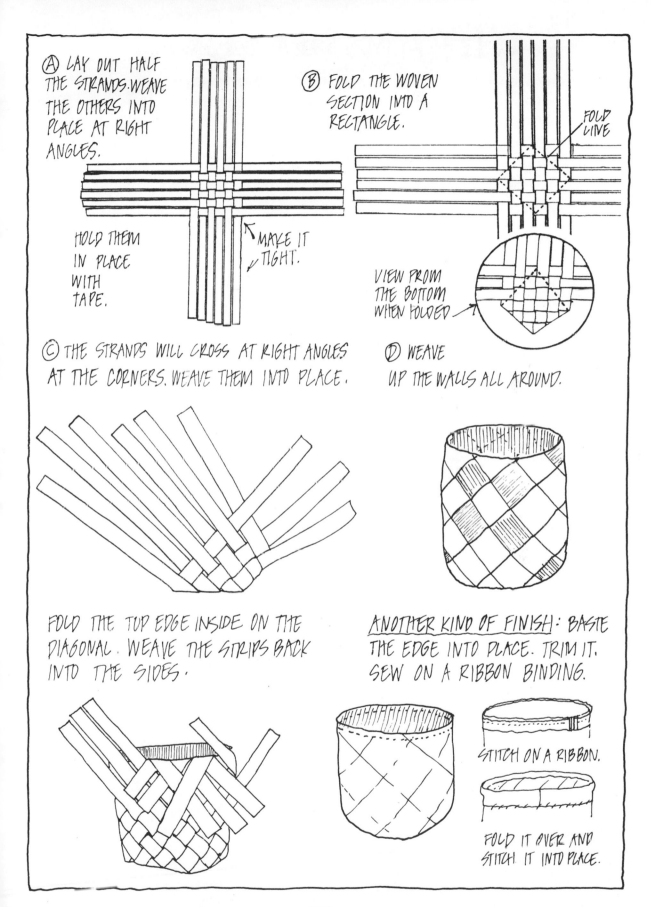

Ⓐ LAY OUT HALF THE STRANDS. WEAVE THE OTHERS INTO PLACE AT RIGHT ANGLES.

HOLD THEM IN PLACE WITH TAPE.

MAKE IT TIGHT.

Ⓑ FOLD THE WOVEN SECTION INTO A RECTANGLE.

FOLD LINE

VIEW FROM THE BOTTOM WHEN FOLDED

Ⓒ THE STRANDS WILL CROSS AT RIGHT ANGLES AT THE CORNERS. WEAVE THEM INTO PLACE.

Ⓓ WEAVE UP THE WALLS ALL AROUND.

FOLD THE TOP EDGE INSIDE ON THE DIAGONAL. WEAVE THE STRIPS BACK INTO THE SIDES.

ANOTHER KIND OF FINISH: BASTE THE EDGE INTO PLACE. TRIM IT. SEW ON A RIBBON BINDING.

STITCH ON A RIBBON.

FOLD IT OVER AND STITCH IT INTO PLACE.

DREAM PILLOWS

Victorians sometimes slept with a little pillow containing a special mixture of herbs that was purported to promote dreaming. It is uncertain whether these pillows actually induced dreaming or just allowed a sleeper to remember a dream better. Make one and find out for yourself. They are a beautiful way to use scraps of ribbon. If you're not interested in improving your night life, fill it with fragrant herbs. It's a very pretty way to scent your drawers.

You Will Need

A piece of satin or taffeta large enough to make two rectangles, 6 inches by 8 inches.

How to Do It

1. Cut two satin or taffeta rectangles, 6 inches by 8 inches. You might use an old dress lining.
2. Cut a number of 6-inch lengths of ribbon. Lay the strips across the rectangle, letting the edges touch. Stitch them in place at both ends.
3. Cut several 8-inch lengths. Weave one through the vertical ribbons in an under-over fashion. Push it to one side and pin it in place. Weave the next length in an over-under fashion.
4. Continue weaving until the space is full. Baste around the outside to hold everything in place.
5. Stitch the front and back pieces around the outside with a 1/4-inch seam allowance, leaving an opening. Turn it right side out.
6. Stuff the pillow with the herbs of your choice. Stitch the opening shut.

> "Economy, the poor man's mint; extravagence, the rich man's pitfall."
>
> M.F. Tupper, 1838

STITCH THE SHORT RIBBONS ACROSS THE RECTANGLE.

WEAVE IN THE LONG RIBBONS.

STITCH THE BACK AND FRONT TOGETHER. CLIP THE CORNERS.

(LEAVE OPEN)

FILL THE PILLOW WITH DREAM POTION. STITCH IT SHUT.

Dream Potion

Mugwort is the main ingredient in this mixture. It's an herb that has long been thought to produce dreams. Folks who believed in the influence of mugwort took a bit of it to sleep with them at night in hopes of adding a little excitement to their night lives.

It's up to you to decide whether or not this mixture of the dreamy stuff and sweet herb causes fantastic dreams. It does produce a nice woodsy scent. To make the dream potion, mix one part mugwort with one part lemon verbena or lemon grass.

ROLLED ROSES

Roses bloom from snips of satin and old silk scarves. Make a single one or a bunch. It takes just a little while to make a whole bouquet of them. You can use them simply as corsages, pin one to a ribbon to wear around your neck, tuck them in your hair, pin a bunch to your hatband, or make several for a garland to grace the crown of a big straw hat.

You Will Need

Silk scarves or satin scraps. Thread and needle.

How to Do It

1. Press the fabric.
2. Make a bias strip of the fabric. If you're using a scarf, fold opposite corners to the center. Fold edges to the center again. If you're using satin, cut a bias strip 3 inches wide and 12 inches long.
3. Begin rolling the strip at one end, making the roll tight at the base and loose at the top to form "petals."

4. Take a few large stitches at the base, tucking the end down to secure the rose roll, and there you have it. "A rose is a rose is a rose."

What to Do with Them

After you've cultivated a rose or two from your scrap pile, you may get the urge to tie one on or to pin one on or tuck one behind your ear. Go ahead. The best part about a silk rag rose is that it never wilts. You'll have a rose that's always full blown day and night.

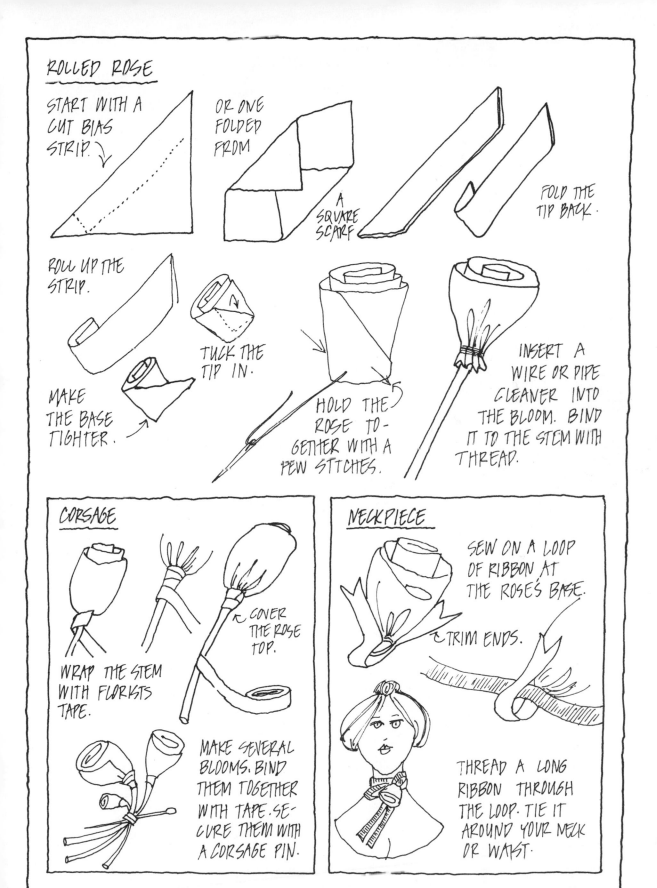

ROLLED ROSE

START WITH A CUT BIAS STRIP.

OR ONE FOLDED FROM A SQUARE SCARF

FOLD THE TIP BACK.

ROLL UP THE STRIP.

TUCK THE TIP IN.

MAKE THE BASE TIGHTER.

HOLD THE ROSE TOGETHER WITH A FEW STITCHES.

INSERT A WIRE OR PIPE CLEANER INTO THE BLOOM. BIND IT TO THE STEM WITH THREAD.

CORSAGE

COVER THE ROSE TOP.

WRAP THE STEM WITH FLORISTS TAPE.

MAKE SEVERAL BLOOMS. BIND THEM TOGETHER WITH TAPE. SECURE THEM WITH A CORSAGE PIN.

NECKPIECE

SEW ON A LOOP OF RIBBON AT THE ROSE'S BASE.

TRIM ENDS.

THREAD A LONG RIBBON THROUGH THE LOOP. TIE IT AROUND YOUR NECK OR WAIST.

You Will Need

Green fabric suitable for leaves.
Liquid laundry starch.

How to Do the Stems

1. Push a pipe cleaner into the base of each rose.
2. Baste stitch around the base of each rose in a circular fashion and pull the stitches taut around the stem. Tie.
3. Begin wrapping the florists tape around the base of each flower. Continue wrapping down the stem, stretching the tape slightly as you go.

How to Do the Leaves

1. Dip the fabric into undiluted liquid starch and hang until the fabric is almost dry.
2. Press damp fabric between two sheets of toweling with an iron until the fabric is dry.
3. Trace a leaf pattern on the fabric and cut it out.
4. Tuck leaf stems into the flower stem as you wrap each one with florists tape.
5. Curl stem ends into tendrils by winding them around a pencil or similar object.
6. Arrange roses together and join them at the stems by wrapping florists tape around them three or so times.
7. Add a pin at this point by wrapping it securely to the stem with florists tape.

> "A cloth kept in an old dust bag near the door is handy to wipe the mud off a dog's paws when he comes in from out-of-doors. He soon learns to wait and hold up his paws till it is done, and much work is saved by teaching him this useful trait."
>
> Good Housekeeping, *1902*

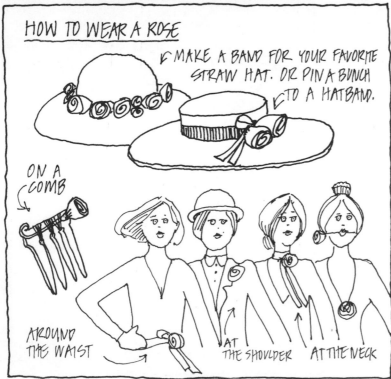

HOW TO WEAR A ROSE

MAKE A BAND FOR YOUR FAVORITE STRAW HAT. OR PIN A BUNCH TO A HATBAND.

ON A COMB

AROUND THE WAIST

AT THE SHOULDER

AT THE NECK

ROSE CORSAGE

When you have passed the heyday of wearing demure neckpieces, even as a costume, consider this corsage. If you aren't the mother of the bride this year, give it to someone who is as a lasting memento.

You Will Need

Pipe cleaners.
Florists tape.
Lightweight florists-type wire.
A brooch or safety pin.
Needle and thread.

ROSE NECKPIECE

For a convincing nineteenth-century touch to any romantic costume, try a rose neckpiece. People will say you are lucky to have a grandmother who saves things.

You Will Need

One rose.
Satin ribbon, 24 inches.
Needle and thread.

How to Do It

1. Snip off a scrap of ribbon about 2 inches long. Make a loop and stitch it to the base of the rose.
2. Thread the remaining ribbon through the loop.
3. You're ready to tie it on. Wrap it twice around your neck and tie in front, beneath the rose.

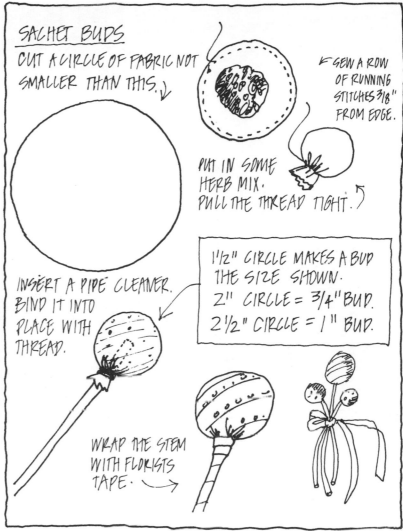

SACHET BUDS
CUT A CIRCLE OF FABRIC NOT SMALLER THAN THIS.

SEW A ROW OF RUNNING STITCHES 3/8" FROM EDGE.

PUT IN SOME HERB MIX. PULL THE THREAD TIGHT.

1½" CIRCLE MAKES A BUD THE SIZE SHOWN.
2" CIRCLE = 3/4" BUD.
2½" CIRCLE = 1" BUD.

INSERT A PIPE CLEANER. BIND IT INTO PLACE WITH THREAD.

WRAP THE STEM WITH FLORISTS TAPE.

SACHET BUDS

These lovely little buds add a little sensual surprise to a corsage. Stuff them with your favorite scented herb or flower. Use these scented buds in the same way that you might use a rolled rose, by putting them on hats or combs or stringing them around your neck. You can also tuck them alongside a bouquet of homemade roses for a little aromatic delight.

You Will Need

A bit of silk, satin, or soft fabric.
Pipe cleaners — as many as there are buds.
Strong thread.
Florists tape.
Sachet.

How to Do It

1. Cut a round of fabric from the pattern.

2. Stuff it with sachet or herbs. Gather up the edges.

3. Insert a pipe cleaner for a stem.

4. Tie the bud around at the base to the stem.

5. Beginning at the base of the bud, wrap down the stem with florists tape.

COMBS

Combs give a pretty touch, tucked up into your hair. If you've never worn combs, you may be delighted to find that they really work. Choose combs from a dime store. They come in several sizes. Be certain that you buy them with the type of teeth shown.

FLOWER COMBS

Here are some little pretties to plant in your hair. You can wear giant ones to cultivate a zany look or tiny blossoms for an effect that's more sedate.

You Will Need

Combs.
Satin roses.
Embroidery floss or fine cord.
White glue.
A small old paintbrush.

How to Do It

Follow the general instructions for satin flowers, beginning with either narrow satin strips or bits of ribbon. Add leaves if you like. The wire stems should be 1 inch long.

1. Place the arrangement of flowers as you like them on the comb.

2. Keeping your arrangement in mind, begin wrapping at one end with floss or cord, leaving about 1/2 inch at the end. Tuck this end under as you wrap.

3. Tuck the flower stems, wrapping loosely as you go, until you reach the end.

4. Tuck the loose end under, then brush the back of the threads with white glue to secure them.

CORDED COMBS

This variation of the comb uses leftover bits of rat-tail cord. If you really want something special, buy some macrame satin cord. About 5/8 yard or 22 inches will do it for a small comb.

You Will Need

Cord.
White glue.
Comb.

How to Do It

1. Begin wrapping, as illustrated, securing the loose end with a drop of glue.

2. Wind twice through each tooth.

3. Secure at the end by tucking the cord tip under already wound ends.

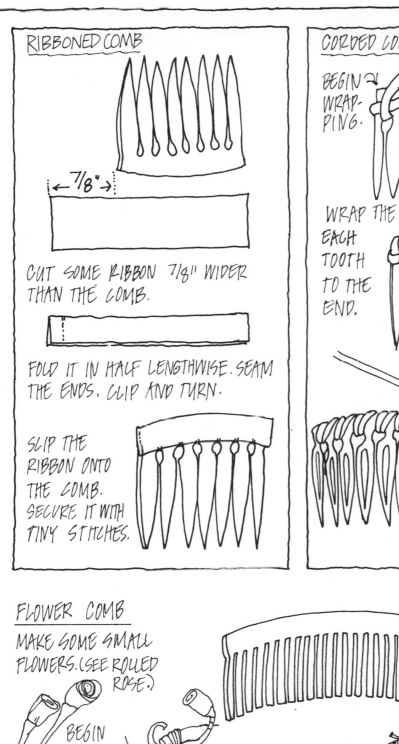

RIBBONED COMB

CUT SOME RIBBON 7/8" WIDER THAN THE COMB.

FOLD IT IN HALF LENGTHWISE. SEAM THE ENDS. CLIP AND TURN.

SLIP THE RIBBON ONTO THE COMB. SECURE IT WITH TINY STITCHES.

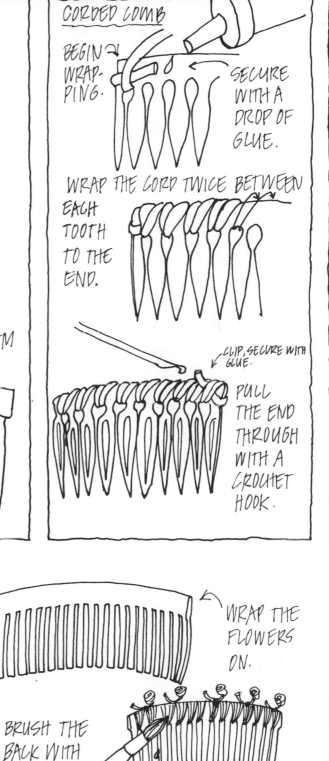

CORDED COMB

BEGIN WRAPPING.

SECURE WITH A DROP OF GLUE.

WRAP THE CORD TWICE BETWEEN EACH TOOTH TO THE END.

CLIP, SECURE WITH GLUE.

PULL THE END THROUGH WITH A CROCHET HOOK.

FLOWER COMB

MAKE SOME SMALL FLOWERS. (SEE ROLLED ROSE.)

BEGIN WRAPPING BY TUCKING THE THREAD ENDS UNDER.

BRUSH THE BACK WITH WHITE GLUE.

WRAP THE FLOWERS ON.

RIBBONED COMBS

These combs are made of little bits of ribbon, embroidered ribbons, or colored ribbons. They make lovely little slashes of color. A bunch of them tucked in your hair can make a rainbow. Embroidered ribbons make special jewellike ornaments.

You Will Need

Ribbon bits.
Combs.
Needle and thread.

How to Do It

1. Measure ribbon to the length of the comb and add 7/8 inch for seam allowance and easement.
2. Fold the ribbon in half lengthwise and stitch each, 3/8 inch from the end.
3. Clip seam corners at an angle, trim edges, and turn.
4. Fit the ribbon piece over the top of the comb. Carefully hand stitch the front ribbon surface to the back surface with tiny running stitches.

VELVET GOWNS

A set of school readers presented by an agent for examination by the principal of a school was condemned after a brief investigation. In one of the primary books this sentence caught the eye of the judge: "Mary has cut her finger; bring a rag." Turning to one of his assistants, the principal said, "Would you teach pupils to use the word 'rag,' when 'piece of cloth' would better express the meaning? 'Rags' is too suggestive of the Italian ragpicker. The word implies something worthless, past use; 'cloth' signifies fabric, something fit for use."

The readers were condemned as being undignified; the man who pronounced the verdict was discriminating in his choice of words; but didn't he ever hear a woman talk about her "dish rags"? That makes me shiver, just as when some people say "young'uns," as though both were necessary evils to be endured with much forbearance. "Dust rags!" the words invariably bring visions of linty, mussy bits of cast-off clothing, on a line with the coats of the two thieves in "Fra Diavolo"; they would leave on the furniture more ravelings and dust than could be removed by them.

Dignify dishcloths, dustcloths, lamp cloths and all pieces of cloth suited to household uses. Sell your old rags; why cumber they the house? Leave rags and tags to the beggars; we prefer velvet gowns.

Good Housekeeping, July 1893

How the Antimacassar Came to Be

Ask anyone what an antimacassar is and you will probably get a blank look. Or you might get a reply like: "Something to prevent fighting and bloodshed." In a sense, the last answer wouldn't be too far wrong. Antimacassars were things our Victorian grandmothers used to prevent the furniture from being massacred by something called Macassar oil, which gentlemen of the time rubbed into their hair. When their heads touched the parlor furniture, the Macassar oil rubbed off, leaving rather unsightly marks and the mistress of the house most distressed.

One of those Victorian ladies invented the antimacassar to prevent such occurrences. They were an immediate success, and every fashionable parlor sported them on the backs and arms of every chair and couch. Ladies' magazines printed endless instructions for making them, and, of course, they were quite in keeping with the spirit of the times that placed glass jars over artificial flowers and heavy drapes over the windows, lest any dust or unabashed sunshine spoil the formal best room of the house.

Given time, every fashion gives way to another. Gentlemen stopped oiling their heads, and heavy curtains were replaced with a delight in sunshine. Eventually the antimacassars were retired to the ragbag along with the dresser scarves and doilies. Who knows? If you open Granny's trunk, you may find a treasure of antimacassars and doilies waiting for you.

SWEET-SMELLING BAGS

You might be the possessor of a drawer full of Grandma's doilies and dresser scarves. They are in the drawer because, well face it, doilies are just not in style and because sentiment prevents you from parting with them. You can turn these precious bits of needlework into sachet bags full of sweet-smelling herbs and spices. They will make Grandma and yourself happy—not to mention your drawers.

If Grandma wasn't kind enough to leave you with a pile of lacies, don't despair. You can find an ample supply of hankies and crocheted pieces at flea markets and junk stores.

Hankie Sachet

Use a hankie or a small scarf.

1. Place the herbs in the middle of the scarf.

2. Bring the four corners together.

3. Tie them in place with a bit of ribbon from your scrap box.

Squares or Rounds

Use a hankie or a small napkin.

1. Fold the piece on the diagonal.

2. Whipstitch the sides together, leaving an opening for stuffing.

3. Stuff it with the scent mixture and finish sewing it shut.

HANKIE SACHET

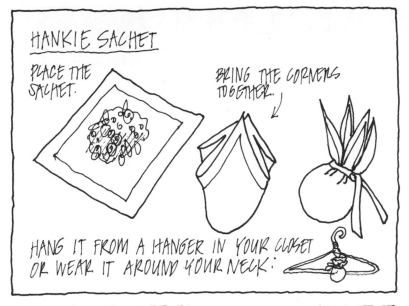

PLACE THE SACHET.

BRING THE CORNERS TOGETHER.

HANG IT FROM A HANGER IN YOUR CLOSET OR WEAR IT AROUND YOUR NECK.

ENVELOPE

START WITH A LONG PIECE WITH A DECORATIVE END.

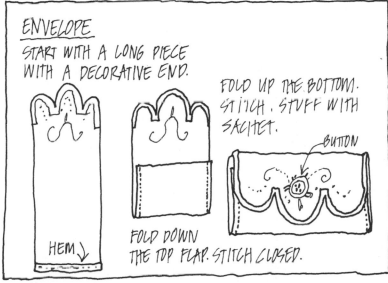

FOLD UP THE BOTTOM. STITCH. STUFF WITH SACHET.

BUTTON

HEM

FOLD DOWN THE TOP FLAP. STITCH CLOSED.

SQUARES OR ROUNDS

START WITH A SQUARE OR A CIRCLE.

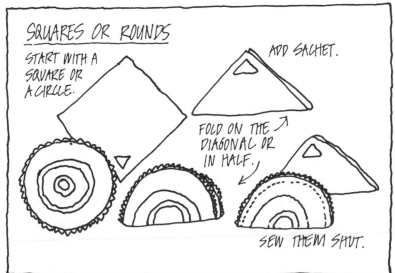

ADD SACHET.

FOLD ON THE DIAGONAL OR IN HALF.

SEW THEM SHUT.

Envelope

Use a long thin piece, like an armchair cover or part of a dresser scarf.

1. Estimate how deep you want the finished piece to be by folding it into thirds. Cut it to size.
2. Turn under the raw edge and sew the side seams shut.
3. Put the herbs into the pocket and whipstitch it shut.
4. Choose a button and sew it through all the layers to close the envelope.

The Ragpicker

The Ragpicker sits and
*   sorts her rags:*
Silk and homespun and
*   threads of gold*
She plucks to pieces and
*   marks with tags;*
And her eyes are ice
*   and her fingers cold.*

The Ragpicker sits in the
*   back of my brain;*
Keenly she looks me
*   through and through.*
One flaming shred I
*   have hidden away —*
She shall not have my
*   love for you.*

Frances Shaw,
The New Poetry, *1932*

SCENTS AND SACHETS

Scents are, well, indefinable really. Not to say there aren't scents that smell like pine or lemon, but some scents smell like nothing really but themselves. No doubt you have a few favorite scents. Possibly they remind you of something—oatmeal cookies or roses, licorice or wintergreen-scented school paste. Sachets are strictly whatever tickles your fancy—amusement pieces.

RECIPES

The sachet recipes that follow are of two basic types: the kitchen sachets and the traditional sachets. For the kitchen sachets, let your nose take a stroll through the kitchen spices to conjure up some appealing mixtures of scent. The traditional sachets find their origins in old herbal books. They are composed of more exotic ingredients that you'll probably find in your local health-food store.

Kitchen Sachet

3 tea bags or 3 tablespoons black tea.
1 tablespoon crushed cinnamon bark.
1/8 teaspoon of ground ginger.
3 crushed cloves or 1/8 teaspoon of ground cloves.

Sleep Potion

2 handfuls of dried rose petals.
1/2 cup mint.
1/4 cup cloves.

Rose Sachet

4 ounces of rose petals.
2 ounces of sandalwood shavings.
1/2 teaspoon rose oil.
  Mix all together.

Lavender Sachet

8 ounces of lavender flowers.
1 1/2 ounces powdered benzoin gum
A few drops of lavender oil.

Verbena Sachet

2 parts lemon verbena.
1 part orange peel.
1 part lemon.

A few crushed cloves (optional).
A small piece of cinnamon bark or some crushed caraway (optional).

PURSE

Lacy crochet work needs to be lined to keep the herbs from leaking out. Choose fabric that is fairly lightweight so that the scent can ooze out. Contrasting colors are very pretty.
1. Cut a circle and stitch it to your doily.
2. Weave a ribbon in and out of the holes next to the edge.
3. Put the herbs in the center and pull the ribbon tight.
4. Tie it shut.

PILLOWS OR CUSHIONS

This way you apply the needlework to a little cushion as the decoration. The fabric should be substantial, so use something like velvet or satin.
1. Cut two pieces of fabric, slightly larger than your lace original.
2. Neatly sew the lace piece onto the right side of the fabric piece you have just cut.
3. Right sides together, stitch around the edge. Use a 1/4-inch seam allowance. Leave an adequate opening for stuffing.
4. Clip and turn it right side out.
5. Add the stuffing. Sew the opening shut.

> "When the trumpets sound, the savage's knife is drawn at the rich man's throat; the poor man's rags are an amulet of safety."
>
> *Phaedrus, 25 B.C.*

CUSHION

START WITH A DOILY. CUT TWO CIRCLES 1/2" LARGER THAN THE DOILY.

SEW THE SIDES TO MAKE A CUSHION. BASTE ON A DOILY. STUFF WITH SACHET.

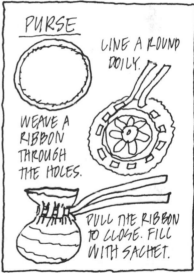

PURSE

LINE A ROUND DOILY.

WEAVE A RIBBON THROUGH THE HOLES.

PULL THE RIBBON TO CLOSE. FILL WITH SACHET.

Doily

The doily (sometimes spelled doyly or doyley) was named after its originator, Sir John D'Oyley, an English merchant and manufacturer. Sir John was in the business of making small ornamental fringed napkins usually woven in colors. They were sometimes used as an ornamental mat or centerpiece.

G.S. Cole,
Encyclopedia of Dry Goods,
1900

COVERED BOOKS

A cloth-covered book is nice to have or to give. It is a good way to use small amounts of those very special fabrics. Choose thick blank books from artist's supply stores to use for a journal or for your collection of family recipes. Thin, lined books from the stationer's make nice memo books. And a new cloth cover will improve any tattered old address book.

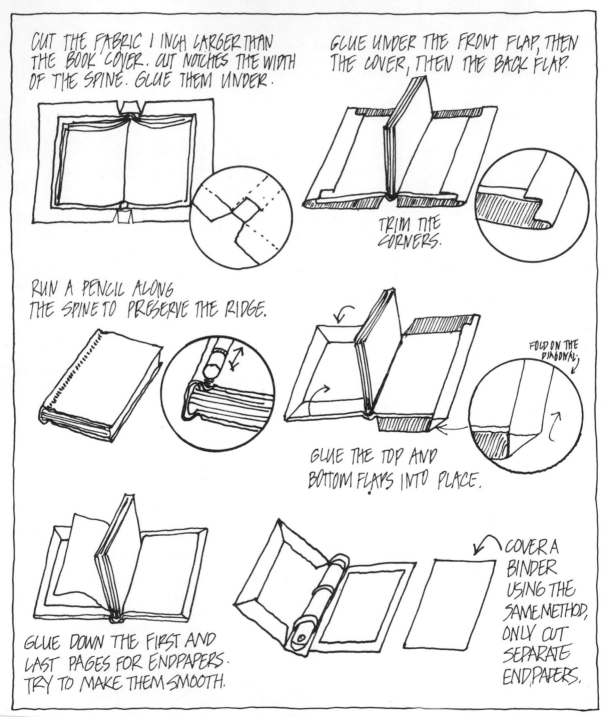

CUT THE FABRIC 1 INCH LARGER THAN THE BOOK COVER. CUT NOTCHES THE WIDTH OF THE SPINE. GLUE THEM UNDER.

GLUE UNDER THE FRONT FLAP, THEN THE COVER, THEN THE BACK FLAP.

TRIM THE CORNERS.

RUN A PENCIL ALONG THE SPINE TO PRESERVE THE RIDGE.

FOLD ON THE DIAGONAL

GLUE THE TOP AND BOTTOM FLAPS INTO PLACE.

GLUE DOWN THE FIRST AND LAST PAGES FOR ENDPAPERS. TRY TO MAKE THEM SMOOTH.

COVER A BINDER USING THE SAME METHOD, ONLY CUT SEPARATE ENDPAPERS.

You Will Need

A hardcover book or a ring binder.

Some fabric slightly larger than the book cover (fabrics of heavier weight — like poplin, duck, or denim—work best).

Wheat paste or white glue.

Heavyweight endpapers if you are covering a binder.

To Prepare the Paste or Glue

Pour paste into 1/3 cup of water slowly, stirring until it's the consistency of thick cream. For glue, thin it with water to the same consistency.

How to Do It

1. Cut fabric to fit the cover of the book. Allow 1 inch all around. Don't forget to count the spine in your measurements.

2. Cut notches for the spine and glue them down.

3. Glue fabric to the book, starting at the spine and working out toward the edges. Paint glue on the book and glue the fabric on, smoothing it with your hand.

4. Apply fabric to the front cover and inside flaps. Smooth and stretch as you go. Do the same for the back.

5. Clip the corners and glue down the top and bottom flaps in front and back.

Endpapers

This is a finishing technique. You can do it two ways.

1. Glue down the first and last pages of the book to the covers to finish.

2. Or use some decorative heavy paper, cut to the size of the covers. Apply these endpapers with rubber cement to prevent wrinkling.

To get rid of an enemy, put nine shoe tacks of the enemy with nine pepper pods in a rag; tie the rag to a lightwood stick; put the stick in running water; and the enemy will leave the country.

Keep a supply of clean woolen rags. Make a smudge of the rag and hold the cut over the smudge to prevent lockjaw.

Tobacco smoke puffed into the ear until the head is plumb chockfull, then stopped up in there with red woolen rags is a speedy relief from pains in the neck.

Current Superstitions,
American Folklore Society,
1896

STUFFED DRAWINGS

There are all sorts of occasions for a stuffed drawing. A big, fat, flabby heart is a wonderful valentine. It's a great way to immortalize your child's drawings. A couple of floppy flowers doused with a little cologne make a nifty gift for scenting drawers. Just the right overstuffed symbol, with a safety pin concealed on the back, will give your lapel a little flash. A whole flock of flying cherubs will give your Christmas tree a really heavenly touch. It's hard to think of an occasion where a stuffed drawing wouldn't be welcome.

You Will Need

Fat felt markers. The kind called "sharpies" work well. (Laundry markers are wash proof and they come in colors.)

White or light-colored cloth. Cotton with a smooth surface works best. Old sheets are perfect.

Stuffing.

Dark thread.

How to Do It

1. Draw directly on the cloth. The only constraint is to keep the outline as simple as possible so the stitching won't be difficult. If you can't draw, invite an artist friend to dinner or use the tracing method: Put the cloth over an original drawing. Trace the design on the cloth. Too faint? Trace the design onto tracing paper with a heavy marker. Place cloth over it. Trace it through.

2. Cut out two shapes.

3. Turn right sides together, stitch around edges leaving an opening.

4. Trim the seams; turn the animal.

5. Stuff with polyester batting or sachet.

6. Sew the opening shut.

DRAW A DESIGN ON CLOTH.
COLOR IN THE DESIGN WITH
MARKERS OR CRAYONS.

CUT A FRONT AND BACK. ALLOW 3/8" ALL
AROUND FOR A SEAM ALLOWANCE.

EDGE OF
DRAWING
STITCH HERE.
3/8" SEAM
ALLOWANCE

SEW THE FRONT AND BACK
TOGETHER. CLIP AND TURN.

STUFF.
STITCH
SHUT.

TREAT THE
BACK AS A
DRAWING OR
USE CONTRAST-
ING FABRIC.

TO TRANSFER A DESIGN

DRAW OR FOLD A GRID OVER THE ORIGINAL
DESIGN. USE A PHOTOCOPY OR A
TRACING IF YOU CAN'T MARK THE
THE ORIGINAL.

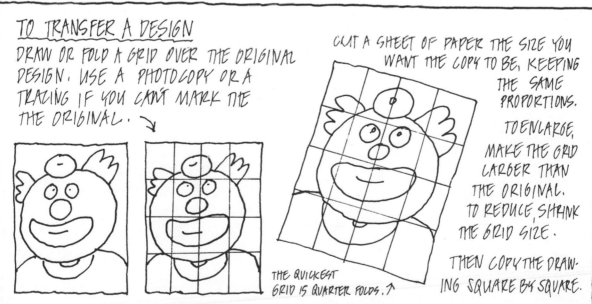

CUT A SHEET OF PAPER THE SIZE YOU
WANT THE COPY TO BE, KEEPING
THE SAME
PROPORTIONS.

TO ENLARGE,
MAKE THE GRID
LARGER THAN
THE ORIGINAL.
TO REDUCE, SHRINK
THE GRID SIZE.

THEN COPY THE DRAW-
ING SQUARE BY SQUARE.

THE QUICKEST
GRID IS QUARTER FOLDS.

Ragbag

"The family ragbag of the old time housekeeper was very different from anything seen to-day. An old bedtick was used oftentimes — or a grain bag of sufficient capacity to hold the rapidly accumulating collection that in due season would be exchanged largely for tinware. When bright calico gowns (homemade) were good enough for Sunday best and red flannel underwear (homemade) was universally worn, the contents of the family ragbag did not lack in color at least."

"The Potentiality of the Old Time Ragbag," Contributors' Club, *Atlantic Monthly*, 1905

DRAWING ON CLOTH

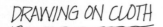

FOR OUTLINES USE PERMANENT FELT MARKERS OR INDIA INK AND A PEN FROM ART SUPPLY.

USE FABRIC CRAYONS FOR LINE AND COLOR. REGULAR CRAYONS WILL WORK IF THEY ARE PRESSED WITH A HOT IRON BETWEEN NEWSPAPERS.

FABRIC DYE WORKS WELL FOR FILLING IN AREAS. USE VARIOUS SIZE BRUSHES TO CONTROL THE COLOR.

TO COPY A DRAWING

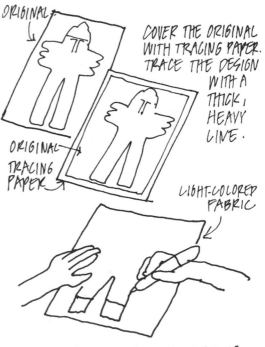

ORIGINAL

COVER THE ORIGINAL WITH TRACING PAPER. TRACE THE DESIGN WITH A THICK, HEAVY LINE.

ORIGINAL

TRACING PAPER

LIGHT-COLORED FABRIC

PUT THE CLOTH OVER THE TRACING NOW TRACE THE DESIGN ONTO THE CLOTH.

THE CHIFFONIERS OF PARIS

Ragpickers' Town reminded me of some ancient tumbledown fishing village, and certainly it was hard to realize that this was positively the city of Paris at the end of the nineteenth century . . . Many of the houses boasted of but one room, in which were, often, neither furniture nor bedding; a bundle of rags did duty for the latter, and in truth it was a case of rags, rags, raggedest of rags everywhere. The ragpickers were seated on their thresholds, or as near the door or apology for a window as it was possible to get. Here and there an ancient chiffonier was patching together old remnants, but most of the men were classifying their merchandise spread upon the floor. The white rags had to be sorted from the colored, and the silk from the cotton or woolen . . .

They were a tough enough looking set, on the whole, but most of the older women appeared to suffer with inflamation of the eyes, and many of the children also — a thing easily to be accounted for by a glance at their grimy hands. Though irredeemably dirty yet the children looked bright, happy, and healthful. And they had reason to, living as they were in an open quarter of low houses, where the sun could stream down on them and the air play around them — a sensation rarely to be experienced in the narrower Paris streets where the immense height of the apartment houses keeps off, for the greater part, these two most important health factors.

This was once the Chateau of Bellevue, which up till 1848 was surrounded by its park of 10,000 square meters. After that date, Monsieur Dore cut the ground up into little lots, and let it out to horticultural-loving Parisians . . .

An enterprising chiffonier not only rented one of these, but with the aid of sardine boxes filled with clay, bits of old building material and tin, built himself a hut. He was the envy of all the crowd of chiffonier friends who came to wonder and admire, and who were not long in following suit. They formed themselves into an independent republic to the number of 400, which by 1860 had increased to between two and three thousand.

Drink is their besetting sin . . . But though a liberty loving race, these wild men and women of the outskirts are a peaceloving one too, and they are seldom in prison; yet from the beginning of their history they have been subjected to every kind of persecution.

"Chiffoniers of Paris,"
Scientific American, 1895

WALLETS

Tie these simple small bags around your waist or wear them like jewelry around your neck. They can even keep your little treasures tidy in a larger bag. Make them in a melange of calico for every day or from satin scraps with decorative button clasps for fancy occasions.

You Will Need

Some cotton scraps.
A small piece of batting.
A shank button and braid or some velcro.

How to Do It

1. Cut two pieces from the pattern — one for the lining and one for the outer wallet. Different fabrics are most interesting.
2. Cut two pockets and one piece of quilt batting.
3. Stitch batting to the wrong side of lining.
4. Hem the flat edge of the pockets by turning it twice.
5. Position pockets atop the lining and baste them in place along outer edges of lining.
6. Pin lining and outer wallet, right sides together. Insert loop and strap ends in the center (see diagram) and stitch, leaving a 2-inch section open.
7. Clip curves and turn. Then whipstitch the opening closed.
8. To finish the wallet, fold it in half and sew on a pretty button.

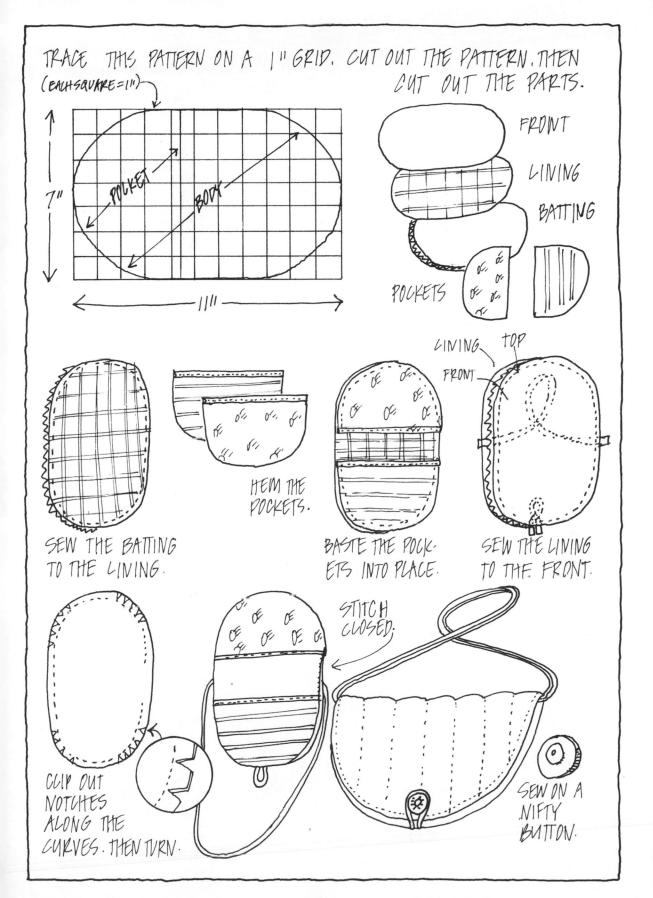

TRACE THIS PATTERN ON A 1" GRID. CUT OUT THE PATTERN. THEN CUT OUT THE PARTS.

(EACH SQUARE = 1")

7"

POCKET

BODY

11"

FRONT

LINING

BATTING

POCKETS

SEW THE BATTING TO THE LINING.

HEM THE POCKETS.

BASTE THE POCKETS INTO PLACE.

LINING

TOP

FRONT

SEW THE LINING TO THE FRONT.

STITCH CLOSED;

CLIP OUT NOTCHES ALONG THE CURVES. THEN TURN.

SEW ON A NIFTY BUTTON.

6

Raggedy Toys

DAISY WAS OUR DOG. Daisy had a thing about rags. Actually it wasn't the rags. She wouldn't have given a mile-high pile of rags a second look. However, wave a rag in her direction and she would transform herself from a mild-mannered mutt to a wild, frothing-at-the-mouth, running, leaping beast bent on capture and destruction. Rags to her were a game.

The wave of a rag, or anything resembling a rag, was a signal for the game to begin. She would spring into action, leaping and snapping until she had the rag firmly in her grip. A spirited tug-of-war would ensue with each of us doing our best to take the rag by force. Daisy had a strategy of yanking and pulling on her end, gradually moving up the length of the material, until finally her opponents would let go rather than face the prospect of dog slobber all over their fingers. When she made a successful grab for the rag, she would run all over the yard shaking it seductively with her kid opponents in hot pursuit. Of course the battle could go the other way with the two-legged team snatching the prize, in which case they would be relentlessly chased until she had attached herself firmly to the end of the rag and another round of tug-of-war commenced. The game was over when the rag had been torn to shreds or when one side collapsed in exhaustion. Usually this was the two-legged side.

We had discovered what kids and other imaginative people in various parts of the world have known for centuries. Rags make good toys. There is sack racing and pillow fighting, flag football and all day games of capture the flag. Rag dolls have been made since the beginning of cloth. Rags have been banners. Rags have been blindfolds for games like blindman's buff. In Spain kids toss a raggy man around in a game called *Pelele*. Eskimo kids toss each other around in a game called *Nalukukatok*. Not to mention resorting to the ragbag for a new identity on occasions like Halloween when a person can transform himself into a sheet spirit or the mummy with throwaway threads.

The wonderful truth is that you can do anything you want to a rag. You can be silly with a rag. Or serious. Or mean. You can cut one up or poke holes in it. Let the dog drag it around the yard. Bury it, or wear it, or tear it, and nobody cares because, well, it's a rag. They can be whatever you want them to be. The neat thing is that you can't hurt a rag. They are raw materials with no restrictions on them. With a rag you have perfect freedom to fool around, which is precisely what the spirit of play is all about.

WINDSOCKS

Windsocks are not just for weathermen. A group of these bright tubes look lovely blowing in the wind in anybody's backyard. Little kids love them; strangers stop and stare and ask you why they are there. They can add as much color to your yard as a bunch of spring flowers. Tightly woven synthetic fabric will make a perfect windsock. Lining fabrics, pieces of parachute from the surplus store, or sleeping-bag scraps are the best materials for windsocks.

You Will Need

Fabric scraps, the more weatherproof the better.
Flexible twigs or pieces of reed.
Bamboo or wooden stakes.
Lightweight string.

How to Do It

1. To make a large-sized sock, cut a rectangle 34 inches by 21 inches. For a smaller size, cut a rectangle 24 inches by 16 inches, or choose your own dimensions. If you don't have a scrap this large, stitch together several scraps of assorted colors to form a piece large enough.
2. Fold the rectangle so that the fold line extends along the length and stitch together.
3. Make a casing 3/8 inch from the edge of the end that is to be the mouth. Leave an opening so that you can insert the reed which will hold the mouth open.
4. Measure the reed so that it is one and a half times the circumference of the windsock's mouth. Insert it into the casing.
5. Thread a piece of string through the mouth with a needle. Attach it to opposite sides of the mouth.
6. Tie the string bridle to the tip of your stake. Cut the bottom of the stake at a slant.

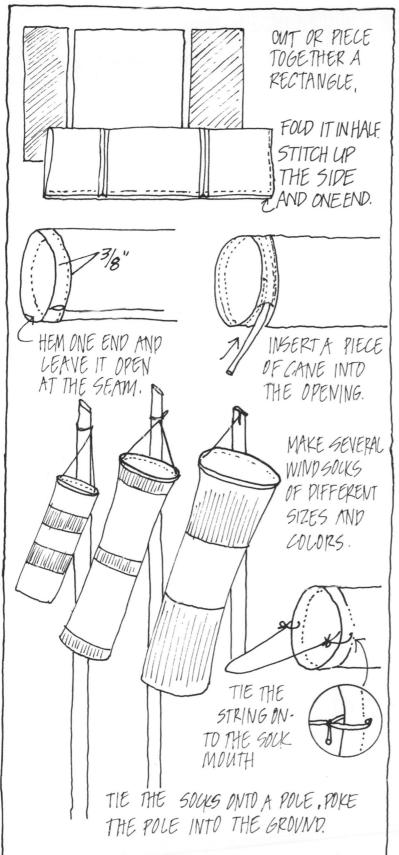

CUT OR PIECE TOGETHER A RECTANGLE.

FOLD IT IN HALF. STITCH UP THE SIDE AND ONE END.

3/8"

HEM ONE END AND LEAVE IT OPEN AT THE SEAM.

INSERT A PIECE OF CANE INTO THE OPENING.

MAKE SEVERAL WIND SOCKS OF DIFFERENT SIZES AND COLORS.

TIE THE STRING ON-TO THE SOCK MOUTH

TIE THE SOCKS ONTO A POLE, POKE THE POLE INTO THE GROUND.

Hanging Out

Once a year, a fascinating collection of sheets, chemises, and union suits flies over the main street of Angels Camp, a small town in the Sierra foothills of California. These lines of limp laundry hang around town for two weeks, adding atmosphere for the Calaveras County Fair and Jumping Frog Jubilee. Townsfolk vie with each other to see who can create the best arranged, most eye-catching string of authentic mining-camp laundry. Prizes are awarded by the judges. This custom marks a celebration that is even more peculiar – the International Frog Jumping Contest. This event is a yearly remembrance of the Mark Twain grudge match, a frog-jump story that is said to have taken place in this town during its rip-roaring mining-camp days.

Martha, First Lady of Thrift

There are several stories or legends told about Martha Washington that would qualify her for the Thrift Hall of Fame. The Washingtons lived the life of the Virginia gentry on the Potomac River. Nonetheless Martha, it seems, was not a lady to throw away an old thing easily. It is said that she dyed all her old worn and faded silk gowns to new colors. She had them unraveled and the thread wound on bobbins and woven into new fabric. Even the general's worn-out stockings were not overlooked and sometimes underwent a transformation into a new cushion or chair cover.

135

WOOLLY MENAGERIE

Socks can be cut, stuffed, and sculpted into all sorts of weird and wonderful beings. They are easy to make because this soft, stretchable fabric is a forgiving one to work with. What you don't accomplish with the scissors, you can make up for with the stuffing and a few stitches. The results will give you a creature to love or something to hug for a small someone you know.

DUCK

CUT A DUCK FROM A WOOLLY GYM SOCK.

BODY

WINGS

FOLD

CUT THE BILL FROM YELLOW KNIT.

SEW THE BODY, RIGHT SIDES TOGETHER. USE A 3/8" SEAM ALLOWANCE. CLIP AND TURN.

STUFF THE DUCK. OVERSTUFF THE CHEEKS, BREAST.

FINISH WITH EYES, BILL, AND A DUCKY BOW TIE.

LONG-LEGGED CHICKEN

YOU NEED ANOTHER SOCK FOR THE CHICKEN.

CUT THE COMB AND LEGS.

STITCH UP THE LEGS. TURN AND STUFF. SEW THEM TO THE BODY.

SEW THE COMB. TURN, STUFF, AND STITCH IT TO THE HEAD.

INSERT A STICK TO STIFFEN THE NECK.

YARN BINDING

You Will Need

Synthetic stuffing.
Socks.
Needle and thread.
Buttons or beads for eyes.
Assorted bits of trim, like sequins, ribbon, yarn.

Notes on Sewing with Socks

This section has instructions for a number of sock creatures. Each recipe is slightly different, but the basic way of working is the same. Here are a few rules to remember.

You can machine or hand stitch your creatures together. Machine stitching is faster, but hand stitching is good to do in front of the T.V. or in waiting rooms.

Don't use really old socks. The thin places allow the stuffing to show through. If they are too worn, the stretch will have worn out of them, and your beasts will look lumpy.

Socks and stuffing are flexible. Mold and shape them with your fingers. Almost any form can be created by a combination of overstuffing, understuffing, and taking tucks with a needle and thread.

AIRBORNE INSECT

WE USED A PAIR OF STRIPED SOCKS, BUT ANY KIND WILL DO.

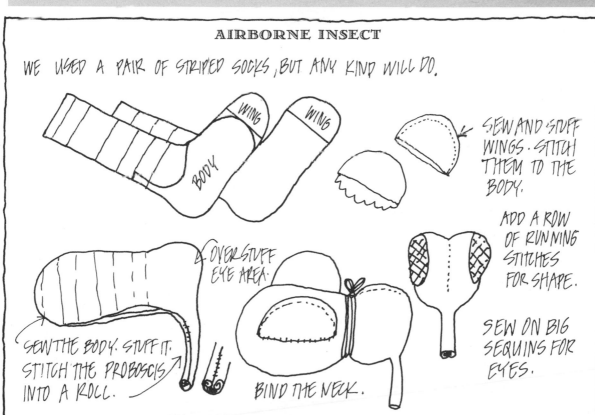

SEW AND STUFF WINGS. STITCH THEM TO THE BODY.

ADD A ROW OF RUNNING STITCHES FOR SHAPE.

SEW ON BIG SEQUINS FOR EYES.

OVERSTUFF EYE AREA.

SEW THE BODY. STUFF IT. STITCH THE PROBOSCIS INTO A ROLL.

BIND THE NECK.

Mystery of the Single Sock

Anyone who has ever folded laundry has puzzled over the phenomenon of the single sock. Socks are always purchased in pairs. And they are always worn in pairs. But they do not stay in pairs. Somehow, somewhere, there seems to be a force operating in the universe that seems to single out socks. This force apparently acts sometime between the moment you peel them off your feet at the end of the day and the time you pull them out of the dryer after the wash. Even though you know that you started with pairs, inevitably at least one sock is not there.

Up to now, no one has shed much light on the mystery of where they go or how this happens. We do know that, like all natural forces, this phenomenon happens to all of us; although this particular force seems to have an affinity for certain ones of us. The best we can do is to offer some suggestions for the use of the sole survivors.

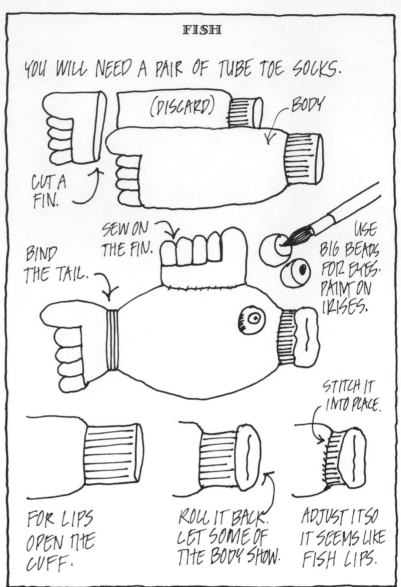

How to Do It

1. For each creature, gather up the materials.
2. Cut them out according to the diagrams. You don't need to be highly exact.
3. With the right sides together, stitch around the edges of the body using a 1/4-inch seam allowance. Use fairly fine stitches. Always leave a section open for stuffing. This is best done in a flat central area.
4. Turn and stuff.
5. Sew the opening shut.
6. Follow the same procedure for the added-on parts like arms and legs.
7. Stitch these to the body with a blind stitch. This part you must do by hand.
8. Now think about adding on the features. Take your time to find eye parts that are exactly right. Experiment with size, color, and placement. Use your imagination. Little differences in this department make a big difference in the finished product.

138

RHINO

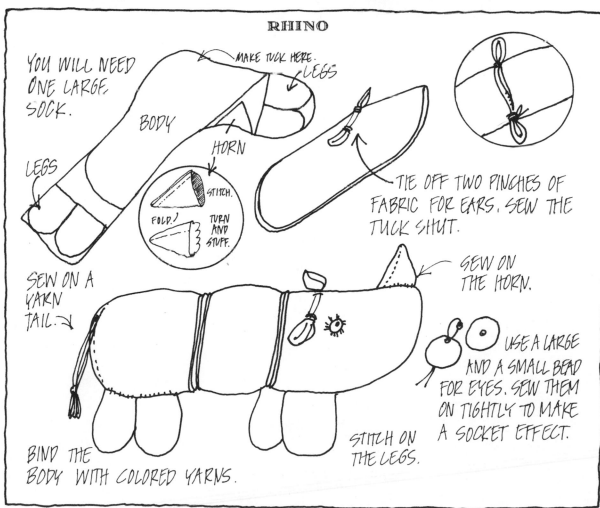

YOU WILL NEED ONE LARGE SOCK.

BODY

LEGS

MAKE TUCK HERE.

LEGS

HORN

FOLD. STITCH. TURN AND STUFF.

TIE OFF TWO PINCHES OF FABRIC FOR EARS. SEW THE TUCK SHUT.

SEW ON A YARN TAIL.

SEW ON THE HORN.

USE A LARGE AND A SMALL BEAD FOR EYES. SEW THEM ON TIGHTLY TO MAKE A SOCKET EFFECT.

STITCH ON THE LEGS.

BIND THE BODY WITH COLORED YARNS.

PRIMAL LIZARD

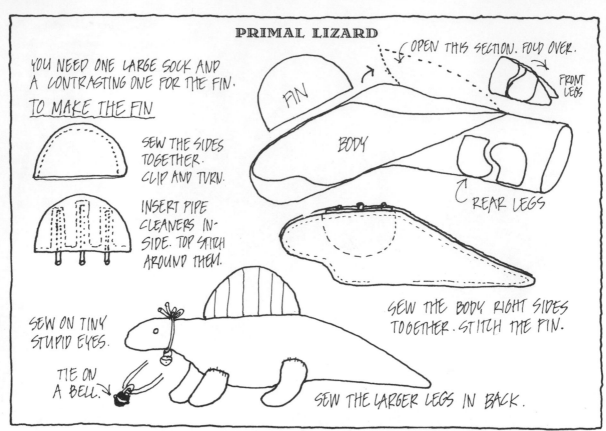

YOU NEED ONE LARGE SOCK AND A CONTRASTING ONE FOR THE FIN.

TO MAKE THE FIN

OPEN THIS SECTION. FOLD OVER.

FIN

BODY

FRONT LEGS

REAR LEGS

SEW THE SIDES TOGETHER. CLIP AND TURN.

INSERT PIPE CLEANERS INSIDE. TOP STITCH AROUND THEM.

SEW THE BODY RIGHT SIDES TOGETHER. STITCH THE FIN.

SEW ON TINY STUPID EYES.

TIE ON A BELL.

SEW THE LARGER LEGS IN BACK.

Rainy Day Rags

Permission to empty a full bag on the garret floor, with liberty to appropriate a reasonable amount of treasure — what more could children ask when a rainy day shut them within doors? How greedily we delved into the mountain of rags, bringing forth such rare finds for our dolls' wardrobes, our patchwork, such fine stuff for horse-reins, and wealth of materials for long, long gay kite-tails! How we bargained for exchange, pillaged each other's piles, played at snow storms with white clippings, and transformed blue jean aprons and ragged trousers into royal robes! There was nothing we could not become with those rags, brides, "injuns," circus horses, clowns in motley — anything. But best of all were the burials, ... Such lovely graves could be fashioned from rags.

"The Potentiality of the Old Time Ragbag,"
Contributors' Club,
Atlantic Monthly, 1905

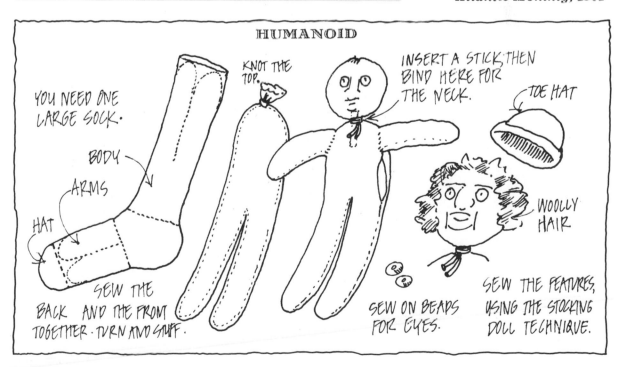

HUMANOID

YOU NEED ONE LARGE SOCK.

BODY

ARMS

HAT

SEW THE BACK AND THE FRONT TOGETHER. TURN AND STUFF.

KNOT THE TOP.

INSERT A STICK, THEN BIND HERE FOR THE NECK.

TOE HAT

WOOLLY HAIR

SEW ON BEADS FOR EYES.

SEW THE FEATURES, USING THE STOCKING DOLL TECHNIQUE.

SNAKE

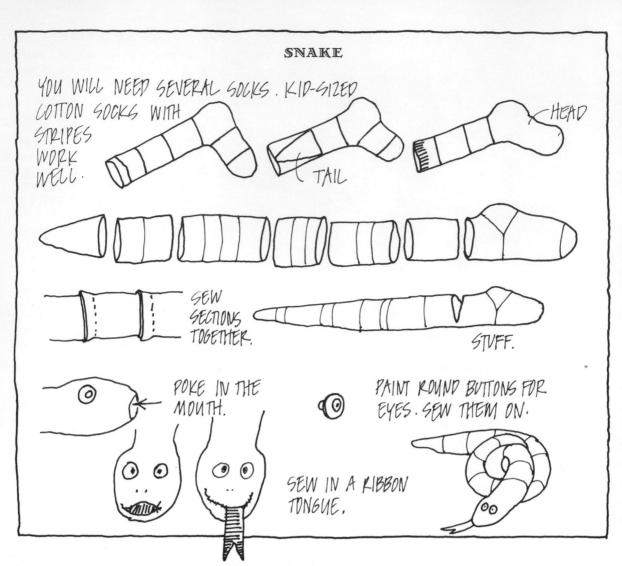

YOU WILL NEED SEVERAL SOCKS. KID-SIZED COTTON SOCKS WITH STRIPES WORK WELL.

HEAD

TAIL

SEW SECTIONS TOGETHER.

STUFF.

POKE IN THE MOUTH.

PAINT ROUND BUTTONS FOR EYES. SEW THEM ON.

SEW IN A RIBBON TONGUE.

Rag Doll

I first saw her sitting among the stalls and clutter. She cost a quarter at a flea market. She was a bit homely — no actually, she was a little scary, with her uneven features and her woolly black hair. She had been used, no doubt about that. This aging lady had seen better days. I turned her over and she spoke to me. Sewn in her back seam was a tag that was written in fading ink. It read: made for Elizabeth, 1932, my name is Betty. This rag lady had a history. It was on the strength of her introduction that I bought her. *Linda.*

"My mother had a room like that. It was full of scraps of material, old newspapers, and had all kinds of stuff on the walls. The dryer was in there. We used to watch T.V. in there. It was awful. There was stuff falling off the shelves! It used to drive my father nuts. That room is probably the reason that I still hate T.V."

Interview with Jim Robertson, March 1978

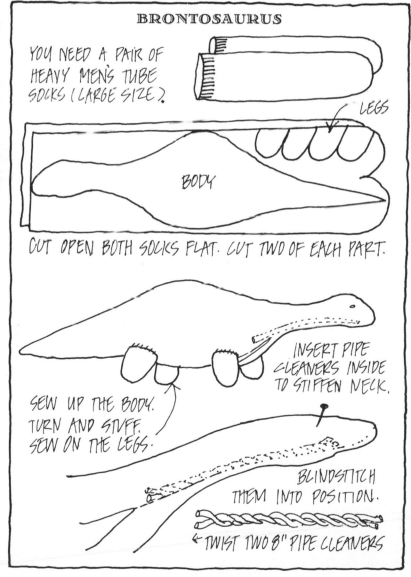

BRONTOSAURUS

YOU NEED A PAIR OF HEAVY MEN'S TUBE SOCKS (LARGE SIZE).

LEGS

BODY

CUT OPEN BOTH SOCKS FLAT. CUT TWO OF EACH PART.

INSERT PIPE CLEANERS INSIDE TO STIFFEN NECK.

SEW UP THE BODY. TURN AND STUFF. SEW ON THE LEGS.

BLINDSTITCH THEM INTO POSITION.

← TWIST TWO 8" PIPE CLEANERS

SOCK~STICK ANIMALS

You might know a small cowboy or cowgirl who needs a sock-stick horse to romp around with. Or they might be more interested in an alligator or a unicorn. If you are a very imaginative person, you might even invent the first sock-stick starship.

You Will Need

An old sock.
Polyester stuffing.
Buttons or beads for eyes.
Needle and thread.
Upholstery tacks and hammer.
Ribbons or heavy yarn for reins.
Scraps of felt.
A dowel or broom handle for stick body, cut to 3 feet in length and painted.

How to Do It

1. Stuff the sock with filling. Leave the cuff only slightly stuffed.

2. Paint the broom handle.

3. Push the stick up into the "neck" to the top of the head or the heel of the sock. Finish packing the stuffing around the neck of the critter.

4. Now tack the sock neck into place with tacks and hammer. Then wrap over the neck with yarn to secure the head.

5. Now you are ready to sculpt the face. Take a good look at the faceless sock critter. Think about what kind of features you want him or her to have. Sculpting can be done simply by pulling and pushing till you have the desired contours, then stitching them in place by hand. You'll want to take your time and experiment here for satisfying results.

6. Once you've got the contours in, you can add eyes, teeth, scrap ears, scrap stuffed horns, or a mane of yarn.

7. Give your critter reins by stitching a ribbon band around its nose. Attach ribbon reins securely to either side of this band and tie them at the back.

START WITH A WOOLLY SOCK

STUFF THE TOE.

PUSH IN THE STICK. PACK THE STUFFING FIRMLY AROUND IT.

SECURE THE SOCK TO THE STICK WITH TACKS. THEN BIND IT WITH YARN.

PAINT THE STICK.

ADD THE EYES, EARS, AND MANE (SEE BELOW).

HORSE DETAILS
CUT FELT TRIANGLES FOR EARS.
SEW ON LENGTHS OF YARN MANE.

(TUCK AND STITCH.)

BUTTON EYE

TAKE SOME STITCHES TO MAKE A NOSE RIDGE.

UNICORN DETAILS
CUT A CONE SHAPE FROM GOLD FABRIC. STITCH UP THE SEAM. STUFF. STITCH IT ON.

FOLD

EYES CAN BE CIRCLES OF FELT OR FELT AND BUTTONS.

MAKE THE BRIDLE FROM COLORFUL RIBBON.

MAKE A HEADBAND AND A NOSE BAND.

YOU MIGHT TIE ON SOME BELLS.

SEW ON FANCY BUTTONS OR SEQUINS.

STICK ALLIGATOR

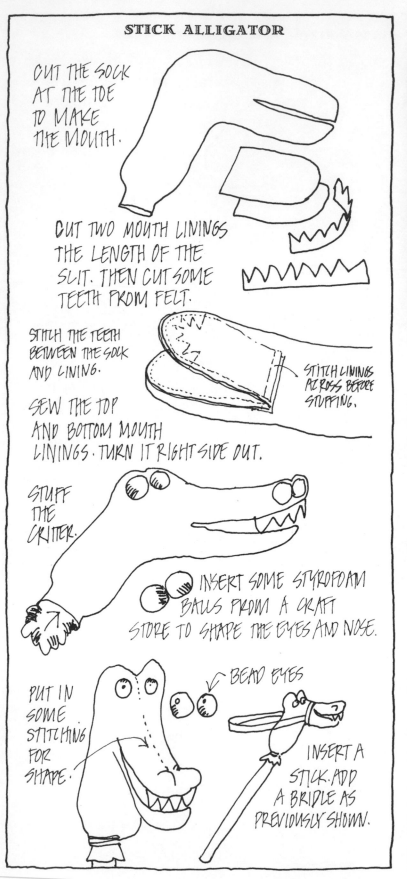

CUT THE SOCK AT THE TOE TO MAKE THE MOUTH.

CUT TWO MOUTH LININGS THE LENGTH OF THE SLIT. THEN CUT SOME TEETH FROM FELT.

STITCH THE TEETH BETWEEN THE SOCK AND LINING.

STITCH LININGS ACROSS BEFORE STUFFING.

SEW THE TOP AND BOTTOM MOUTH LININGS. TURN IT RIGHT SIDE OUT.

STUFF THE CRITTER.

INSERT SOME STYROFOAM BALLS FROM A CRAFT STORE TO SHAPE THE EYES AND NOSE.

PUT IN SOME STITCHING FOR SHAPE.

BEAD EYES

INSERT A STICK. ADD A BRIDLE AS PREVIOUSLY SHOWN.

Stick Horse

When I was five, I wanted a horse desperately. I asked for one in the mornings. And in the afternoons. And in the evenings after watching the Annie Oakley show on T.V. Just before going to sleep, I didn't forget to put in a request to the Almighty.

My prayers were answered in the form of a homemade stick horse. I can't say I wasn't disappointed. In the back of my five-year-old mind, I knew that this was just a temporary situation. So my requests were amended to include the adjective *real* in front of the word *horse*. I had learned the value of asking for things in a precise manner. In the meantime, I settled for riding the range on a stick horse and we got to be good friends. Eventually I did get the real thing, but that was years later. I must admit Stick Horse and I had some good times together, and, as my father pointed out, he was a lot cheaper to feed. *Linda.*

GLOVE PEOPLE

You can make a whole crowd of little folks from an old glove. Make a family, a cocktail party, a group of conspirators, a barbershop quintet, Goldilocks and the Three Bears plus one, or feeding time at the zoo.

USE A LIGHT-COLORED SMOOTH SURFACED GLOVE.

USE A PENCIL TO PUSH IN STUFFING.

BIND NECK.

DRAW ON THE FEATURES WITH A SKINNY MARKER.

ADD DETAILS:

SEW ON FELT MONKEY EARS.

OR POINTY PIG EARS.

SEW ON YARN HAIR.

OR UNRAVELED YARN HAIR.

T-SHIRT YARN TIE

COTTON OR WOOL HAIR

You Will Need

An old glove of tightly woven cotton or synthetic fabric.
A pen that will draw on the fabric.
Some stuffing.
Assorted bits of yarn and trim.

How to Do It

1. Draw a face on the palm side of a glove finger.

2. Push a wad of stuffing to the tips of the finger.

3. Tie off the finger with thread or yarn to make the neck.

4. Add color to the face with the pens. Apply hair, neckties, ears — whatever seems right for your finger person.

5. Do the same for the other four.

6. When you've finished your glove people, make up a play starring your fancy new five fingers. Perform it for an appreciative audience. Anyone six or under is sure to love it. If you're not the dramatic type, you can always wear them to church.

JUGGLING BALLS

These colorful balls can be made from any heavy fabric scraps, but velveteen and corduroy make the most colorful balls. They have a nice feel, but best of all they don't bounce. This saves a beginning juggler a lot of ball-chasing time. Make them for yourself, if you've always had a secret yen to juggle, or as a nifty gift for a nonjuggling friend.

You Will Need

Fabric scraps of several different colors.
Sand or birdseed for filling.
Needle and thread.

How to Do It

1. Cut six sides using pattern.
2. Assemble the sides of the balls by stitching four together to form a rectangle.
3. Join the ends together to form a box.
4. Stitch in top side of box.
5. Stitch in the bottom side of box, leaving one edge open.
6. Turn the cube right side out.
7. Fill the cube with birdseed. Use a funnel to make the job easier. Stuff it as hard as you can. Whipstitch the opening closed.

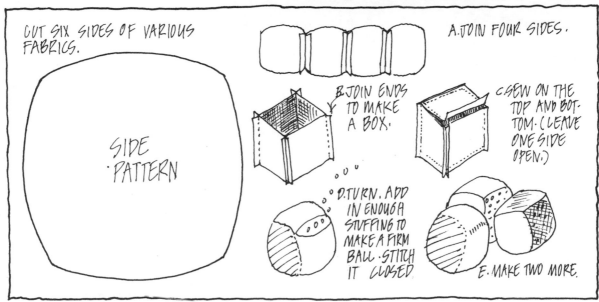

CUT SIX SIDES OF VARIOUS FABRICS.

SIDE PATTERN

A. JOIN FOUR SIDES.

B. JOIN ENDS TO MAKE A BOX.

C. SEW ON THE TOP AND BOTTOM. (LEAVE ONE SIDE OPEN.)

D. TURN. ADD IN ENOUGH STUFFING TO MAKE A FIRM BALL. STITCH IT CLOSED.

E. MAKE TWO MORE.

How to Juggle

1. Get to know your juggling balls by taking a ball in your hand and tossing it about 2 feet into the air. Catch it with the same hand. Practice this until you can do it smoothly.

2. Next practice throwing the ball with your right hand and catching it with your left hand.

3. Toss the ball in a semicircle to your left hand, focusing your eyes on the semicircle as a whole. Do not follow the ball with your eyes. Practice this until you can keep the ball moving smoothly.

4. Take two balls in your right hand, forming a loose cup with your hand. Throw one ball into the air about 2 feet high. As it is beginning to come down, toss the second one up, slightly to its right. Catching the first ball with the same hand, toss it again and catch the second ball. Remember to keep your eyes and attention focused on the whole semicircle.

5. Practice the same pattern using your left hand. After you've mastered both hands, you are ready for juggling three balls.

6. Ready for three balls? Take two of them (Balls A and C) in your right hand and one (Ball B) in your left hand.

7. Toss Ball A up from your right hand to form an arc. As it reaches a point above your left hand, toss Ball B from your left hand to form an arc to your right hand. Catching Ball A in your left hand now toss Ball C from the right hand to arc toward the left hand. This will take lots of practice, so try not to be discouraged if you find yourself dropping the balls at first.

LEARNING HOW TO JUGGLE

1. PRACTICE ONE HANDED.

2. RIGHT TO LEFT AND BACK.

3. WITHOUT LOOKING.

4. TRY TWO BALLS.

5. TWO BALLS (OTHER HAND).

6. NOW FOR THREE.

7. JUGGLE!

7

Rag Notions

ONE AFTERNOON during Christmas vacation, I arrived home unexpectedly from college. I was hoping to startle everyone with a grand entrance. I had gotten a surprise ride home from the north country and no one knew exactly when I was coming.

As I opened the front door and slithered into the house, it didn't take me long to realize that all the activity in the house was in the kitchen. I followed my nose to the good smells and the hustle that was emanating from what seemed like the only occupied room in the house. General confusion and Christmas chaos spilled over everywhere. Mom was clanging and banging and baking. The dog was watching her adoringly, waiting for some crumbs to fall his way. Stella was hunched over the table that was strewn with a sea of colorful bits and pieces. She had a needle in her hand and the cat in her lap — not an unusual pose for Stella. Dad was behind the newspaper, just home from work and doing his best to be oblivious. There was such concentration amid this confusion that I had to drop my bags with an emphatic thump before anyone took note of my momentous arrival.

In the rush of hugs and howdies and how-did-you-get-heres, I didn't notice that those intriguing bits that had engulfed the kitchen table had been whisked away. I didn't notice until Christmas morning when the gifts were unwrapped. From the tissue paper package that Stella handed me emerged a soft voile shirt. It was black with a red yoke that was studded with embroideries and sprinkled with beads and sparkly bits of red and green and yellow. All those fragments from the kitchen table had been put together to make a most wonderful shirt. Stella explained the bits while I put it on. The body had been cut from an old skirt. The yoke was a piece from the voluminous family scrap pile. The embroideries were clipped from fancy tea aprons found at the Goodwill. The beads, sequins, rick-rack, and bits of felt were dredged up from the notions drawer.

Once I put it on, my suspicions were confirmed. This shirt made me feel like Christmas. Indeed, it still does. It is in my collection of special things. I wear it every Christmas with special affection. And sometimes I put it on when I'm in need of a little magic.

Anyone who sews has an inevitable collection of rag notions — bits of ribbons, braids, and beads; little embroideries needled by Aunt Winnie; fragile laces; souvenir patches from exotic places; buttons from an old scout uniform. It's quite a collection. You probably have a whole pile of bits that sparkle and shine hidden away in a drawer that is Christmas just waiting to happen. *Linda.*

BUTTON BROOCHES

Little bits of brocade, small scraps of elegant fabric from the antique store, embroidered doilies from the linen closet, even the appliqued corners of napkins or dresser scarves can be the makings for some really special buttons. In addition to the fabric, all you need is a package of self-cover buttons. They come in a variety of sizes. Pick ones that are appropriate to your embroidered design.

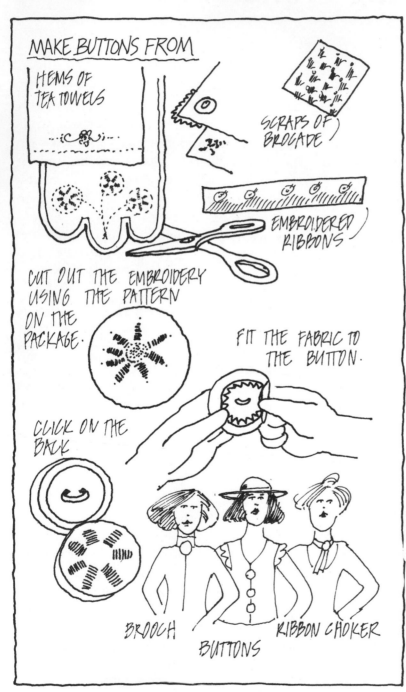

MAKE BUTTONS FROM

HEMS OF TEA TOWELS

SCRAPS OF BROCADE

EMBROIDERED RIBBONS

CUT OUT THE EMBROIDERY USING THE PATTERN ON THE PACKAGE.

FIT THE FABRIC TO THE BUTTON.

CLICK ON THE BACK

BROOCH

BUTTONS

RIBBON CHOKER

You Will Need

Fancy bits of fabric.
Self-cover buttons, measuring half the size of the design you want to mount.

How to Mount Them

Each brand of self-cover buttons requires a slightly different method, so specific instructions are impossible. Just follow the instructions that come with the package.

How to Wear Them

You can wear these buttons as brooches by attaching a pin to the back. Wear them as you would a piece of costume jewelry, or use them as special buttons to adorn a jacket. The remaining bits of embroidery can be used for trim on the garment.

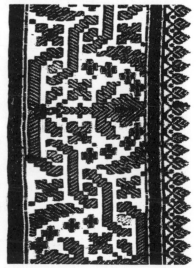

A Fortune in Buttons

In some circles, counting your buttons was a favorite way for young ladies to find out about the feelings of their gentlemen friends. A girl would count on the buttons of her dress, or her boots, "He loves me, he don't; he'll marry me, he won't; he would if he could, but he can't."

These same buttons could tell what profession she could expect her betrothed to be, "Rich man, poor man, beggarman, thief, doctor, lawyer, merchant, chief." Sometimes there was "Tinker, tailor, soldier, sailor."

And if that wasn't enough, the button charm could foretell where the little lady would live, "Big house, little house, pig sty, barn." Of course a person's fortunes would change daily, but so it is with love.

Button Charms

Girls in the late 1800s collected buttons for a very special reason. According to button lore, when a young lady had collected a string or a ribbon holding one thousand buttons, her true love would appear and sweep her off her feet into the blissful state of matrimony. The string had to contain one thousand buttons, each one different. The first button was large, the *touch button,* and had special meaning. It might have belonged to a grandmother or come from the coat of the unsuspecting husband-to-be. The string took a long time to finish; the final button was often delayed if no suitable man was in sight. Very few complete strings have been found; they were probably broken up for mending and sewing on clothes.

BUTTONNIERES

Sometimes you find a button that's more like a jewel than a humble fastener. Here is a way to wear your buttons in a more fanciful fashion. You can turn your buttons into little bouquets to decorate your decolletage or buttonhole or bonnet. Choose a multicolor assortment from your button box. For a more demure bouquet that will catch the light in rainbow colors, choose a bunch of mother-of-pearl buttons.

You Will Need

An assortment of weird and
   wonderful buttons.
Some thin wire.
Florists tape.
Pliers.
A pin.

How to Do It

1. Cut a piece of wire 8 inches long. Double it around.

2. Thread it through the holes of the button.

3. Hold the wire close to the button and twist it until the wire is tight. Continue to wind the wire until its entire length is intertwined.

4. Wrap the wire with florists tape to finish the stem.

5. For a whole bunch of flowers, bind several button blossoms into a bouquet with florists tape.

6. For a buttonniere that you can pin to your lapel, you will need a pin (the kind with a flat back works best). You can get them at a hobby or dime store or by taking apart an old corsage. Bind the pin to the bunch of button flowers with florists tape.

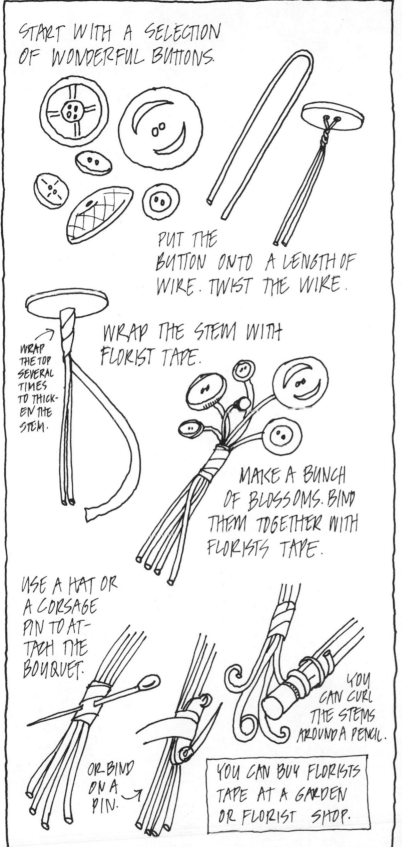

START WITH A SELECTION OF WONDERFUL BUTTONS.

PUT THE BUTTON ONTO A LENGTH OF WIRE. TWIST THE WIRE.

WRAP THE STEM WITH FLORIST TAPE.

WRAP THE TOP SEVERAL TIMES TO THICKEN THE STEM.

MAKE A BUNCH OF BLOSSOMS. BIND THEM TOGETHER WITH FLORISTS TAPE.

USE A HAT OR A CORSAGE PIN TO ATTACH THE BOUQUET.

YOU CAN CURL THE STEMS AROUND A PENCIL.

OR BIND ON A PIN.

YOU CAN BUY FLORISTS TAPE AT A GARDEN OR FLORIST SHOP.

Button Collecting

There was a time when collecting buttons was considered a wacky hobby. These days, however, when people collect barbed wire, beer cans, and whiskey bottles, making a collection of buttons seems perfectly sane. The truth is that button collecting on a serious scale began in the 1930s, when Mrs. Gertrude Patterson went on the radio and described her hobby to America. She said that it was a great hobby for folks with not much money and a lot of time. During the depression years of the 1930s, many people fell into this category. It was an idea whose time had come. Button fever swept the country, and Mrs. Patterson became the acknowledged founder of the movement.

People continue to collect buttons today. There is a National Button Society that sponsors shows and puts out a publication called the *National Button Bulletin.* Society members gather locally to trade information. They discuss button history and classify buttons into groups with names like *goofies* and *aristocrats.* And, of course, they trade buttons.

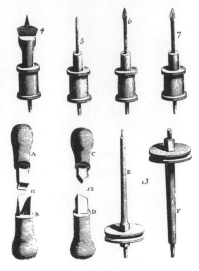

Button Background

The phenomenon of pushing hard little knobs through holes in cloth as a way of holding an article of clothing on the body was not invented until the thirteenth century. The first buttons were worn strictly as ornaments. The Greeks and Etruscans wore them with loops to fasten their tunics.

Later the wild Scottish clansmen wore silver buttons on their jackets as burial insurance. The silver would cover the cost of a proper burial if the warrior was killed in foreign territory.

By the 1700s, buttons were lavished on the clothes of the rich. They were often made of gold or silver and considered more as jewelry than as the utilitarian items they are today. The Puritans, ever on their guard against wild extravagance, were flatly opposed to buttons and passed laws against them in the early days of America. The Amish still fasten their clothes with hooks and eyes in the simple tradition of their forefathers. And, of course, the rest of the world has gotten along splendidly by wrapping, tying, and otherwise avoiding the European invention of the button.

(Above, left) Eighteenth-century artisans making buttons of resin which are then applied to a metal shank.

(Above, right) An assortment of button-making tools.

(Below) These people are making button molds for the casting of metal buttons. Two workers saw out a block of wood. A man and a woman drill the outline of a mold into the wood. The exact pattern is drilled out with the big two-man drillwheel pictured in the background.

Diderot Pictorial Encyclopedia of Trades and Industry

BUTTON CHOKER

At first glance these chokers look like those candy necklaces that you might have nibbled on as a kid. They are, in fact, a long string of buttons on edge. Empty the contents of your button collection onto the rug and choose the materials to make a handsome necklace.

You Will Need

Buttons, 30 to 50 of the same diameter.
Soutache or flat braid, 1/2 yard (the kind that's 1/4 inch wide).
Thread.
Thin wire.
White glue.

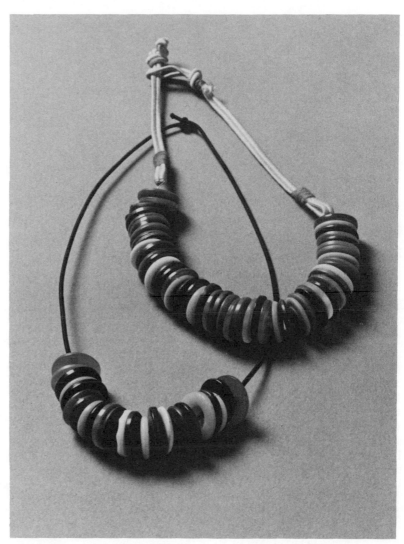

How to Do It

1. Cut a piece of wire about 10 inches long. With pliers, put a loop at one end. Twist the loop several times. Clip off the excess wire.

2. Thread the buttons onto the wire. Arrange them according to color groups, or put single contrasting colors next to each other.

3. Close the other end by putting a loop in the wire.

4. Add on ties of the braid by threading it through the wire loops. Secure the braid loops with a thread binding. (See illustration for details.)

5. Put a triple knot in one tie and a slipknot with a loop in the other tie to fasten the choker.

6. Loop the braid through the wire eyes. Push a stitch through the braid. Wrap the loops closed with a thread. Use a contrasting color.

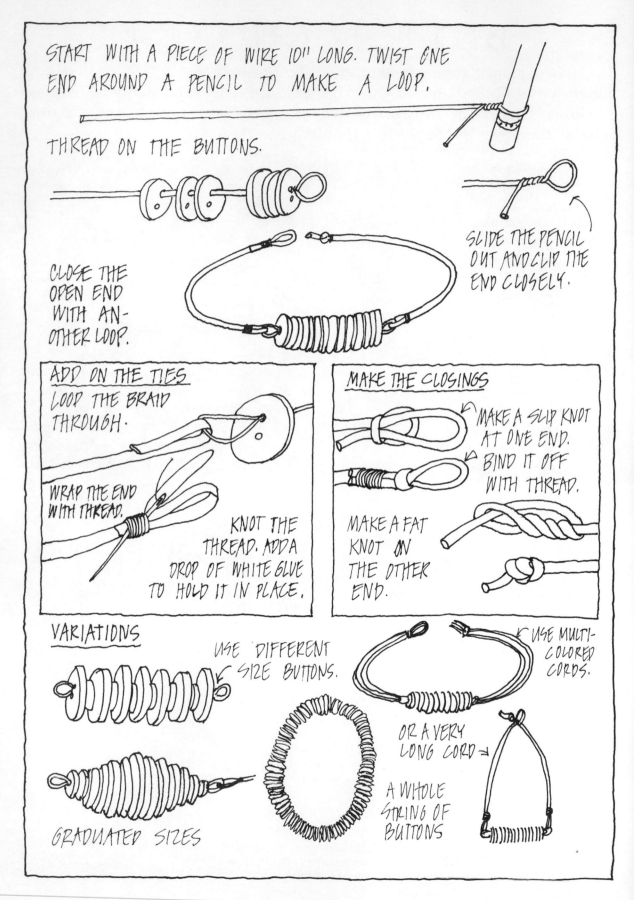

START WITH A PIECE OF WIRE 10" LONG. TWIST ONE END AROUND A PENCIL TO MAKE A LOOP.

THREAD ON THE BUTTONS.

SLIDE THE PENCIL OUT AND CLIP THE END CLOSELY.

CLOSE THE OPEN END WITH ANOTHER LOOP.

ADD ON THE TIES
LOOP THE BRAID THROUGH.

WRAP THE END WITH THREAD.

KNOT THE THREAD. ADD A DROP OF WHITE GLUE TO HOLD IT IN PLACE.

MAKE THE CLOSINGS

MAKE A SLIP KNOT AT ONE END.
BIND IT OFF WITH THREAD.

MAKE A FAT KNOT ON THE OTHER END.

VARIATIONS

USE DIFFERENT SIZE BUTTONS.

USE MULTI-COLORED CORDS.

GRADUATED SIZES

A WHOLE STRING OF BUTTONS

OR A VERY LONG CORD →

The ragpicker worked in silence among the stains and smells. His bag was swelling.

The city turned slowly on its left side, but the eyes of the house remained closed, and the bridges unclasped. The ragpicker worked in silence and never looked at anything that was whole. His eyes sought the broken, the worn, the faded, the fragmented. A complete object made him sad. What could one do with a complete object? Put it in a museum. Not touch it. But a torn paper, a shoelace without its double, a cup without saucer, that was stirring. They could be transformed, melted into something else. A twisted piece of pipe. Wonderful, this basket without a handle. Wonderful, this bottle without a stopper. Wonderful, the box without a key. Wonderful, half a dress, the ribbon off a hat, a fan with a feather missing. Wonderful, the camera plate without the camera, the lone bicycle wheel, half a phonograph disk. Fragments, incompleted worlds, rags, detritus, the end of objects, and the beginning of transmutations . . . Inside the shack rags. Rags for beds. Rags for chairs. Rags for tables. On the rags men, women, brats. Inside the women more brats. Fleas. Elbows resting on an old shoe. Head resting on a stuffed deer whose eyes hung loose on a string . . .

The brats sitting in the mud are trying to make an old shoe float like a boat. The woman cuts her thread with half a scissor.

The ragpicker reads the newspaper with broken specs. The children go to the fountain with leady pails. When they come back the pails are empty. The ragpickers crouch around the contents of their bags. Nails fall out. A roof tile. A signpost with letters missing . . .

The ragpickers are sitting around a fire made of broken shutters, window frames, artificial beards, chestnuts, horses' tails, last year's holy palm leaves. The cripple sits on the stump of his torso, with his stilts beside him. Out of the shacks and the gypsy carts come the women and the brats.

Can't one throw anything away forever? I asked.

The ragpicker laughs out of the corner of his mouth, half a laugh, a fragment of a laugh, and they all begin to sing.

First came the breath of garlic which they hang like little red Chinese lanterns in their shacks, the breath of garlic followed by a serpentine song:

> Nothing is lost but it changes
> into the new string old string
> in the new bag old bag
> in the new pan old tin
> in the new shoe old leather
> in the new silk old hair
> in the new hat old straw
> in the new man the child
> and the new not new
> the new not new
> the new not new.

Anais Nin

BUTTON GAMES AND TOYS

Here is a series of games and toys using nothing more elaborate than a few buttons. You don't play games? Probably you know some young folks who do. It is handy to have a few surprise activities tucked away for the times when you are visited by short people. Nobody likes to see guests bored.

They don't play games unless they are advertised on the television? Probably they would be delighted to learn. It's surprising how much fun a person can have with just simple stuff.

Tiddlywinks

For tiddlywinks you need three medium-sized buttons of the same size and color for each person playing and one more large button. The buttons should be round and as flat as possible. You also need a piece of chalk or a stick for marking lines.

To play, draw a starting line or mark one with a stick. Position the finish line a foot or more away from the start. Each player snaps his three buttons from the start toward the finish by placing the large button atop the edge of the smaller one and pushing down to make it jump. The winner is the player with the most buttons over the finish line.

Button Button

You might remember this game from the days when you were a kid. It is still a favorite with younger children. It has the appeal of being a kind of psychological test and exercise for the players that requires watching, reading body language,

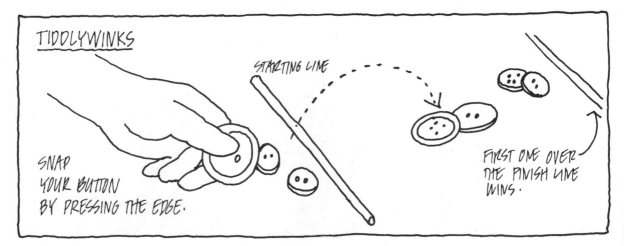

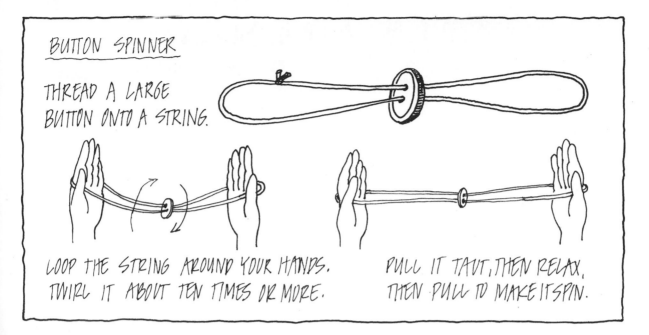

BUTTON SPINNER

THREAD A LARGE BUTTON ONTO A STRING.

LOOP THE STRING AROUND YOUR HANDS. TWIRL IT ABOUT TEN TIMES OR MORE.

PULL IT TAUT, THEN RELAX, THEN PULL TO MAKE IT SPIN.

and practicing a poker face. It is a game of suspense and drama, particularly if you are about six years old. Are you ready for "Button Button, Who's Got the Button?"

The only equipment that you need for this game is a button of a size that can be easily hidden between the palms of the hands. Also you need at least four players. More are even better.

One person is *it*. And another person is the button master. The other players stand around these two in a circle with their hands in prayer position extended in front of them.

The button master conceals the button between his palms. He visits each person in the circle and slips his hands between their folded palms. At some place around the circle, he secretly drops the button into someone's hands. Meanwhile the person who is it watches this operation with hawklike intensity, trying to figure out who's got the button. After every pair of palms has been visited at least once, the button master asks: "Button button, who's got the button?" It has to guess, and if it guesses right, he or she becomes the button master. The person holding the button is now it.

Button Spinner

To make a button spinner, you will need a button that measures an inch or more in diameter with two or four holes. The bigger the better. You also need a length of heavy thread, about 28 inches long.

To assemble the spinner, all you do is thread the string through the first hole and back through the second hole. Tie the thread ends on one side of the button into a knot.

Now you're ready to play with it. Center the button in the middle of the thread. Hold each end of the thread between thumb and forefinger. Wind the thread by flipping the button toward you in a circular fashion just like you would turn a jump rope. Do this about ten times. Then pull evenly and steadily on both sides of the thread to spin the button around. It will unwind and wind, spinning faster and faster, as you relax and tighten the thread. It makes a humming noise as it goes that will delight your young friends. You can paint designs on the button if you like. The colors will blend into new ones as they spin.

LACE FRAMING

Lace doesn't have much of a place in modern life, unless it's along the edges of ladies' underwear, where a little surreptitious luxury is allowed to lurk next to a lady's skin. Although current fashion does feature frills, laces are for special-occasion finery, often worn at weddings where more romantic fashions prevail.

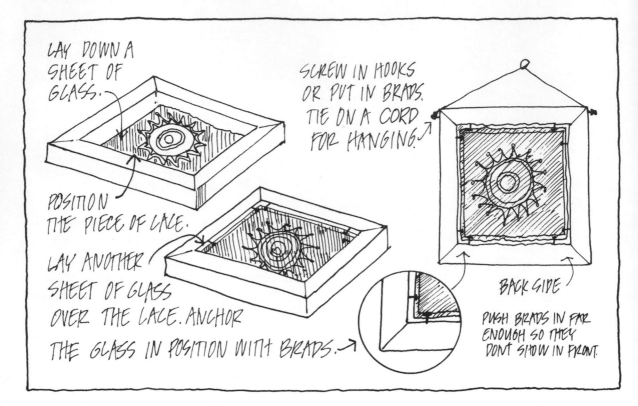

LAY DOWN A SHEET OF GLASS.

POSITION THE PIECE OF LACE.

LAY ANOTHER SHEET OF GLASS OVER THE LACE. ANCHOR THE GLASS IN POSITION WITH BRADS. →

SCREW IN HOOKS OR PUT IN BRADS. TIE ON A CORD FOR HANGING. →

BACK SIDE

PUSH BRADS IN FAR ENOUGH SO THEY DON'T SHOW IN FRONT.

Few people know what to do with lace. As a result, it often turns up at thrift shops or waits tucked away in linen closets.

Perhaps you have a bit of lace that deserves a second look. I like to think of it as a sort of two-dimensional painting with thread. It's astonishing to ponder the number of hours and the skill it took to produce lace.

Lace framing is a perfect way to appreciate and preserve the beauty of lace. Suspended next to a window, lace pieces look like captured snowflakes.

You Will Need

Lace.

A frame of your choice, large enough for the lace.

Two pieces of picture-framing glass cut to the dimensions of the frame. You can buy it at glass suppliers or frame stores.

Some brads or glaziers' points.

Screw hooks.

How to Do It

1. First clean the glass thoroughly.
2. Place one of the pieces of glass in the frame, face down on the work surface.
3. Position the lace on the glass in the frame, taking care not to soil the glass.
4. Place the other piece of glass in the frame, carefully, to sandwich the lace piece. Avoid applying pressure to the glass.
5. Anchor the glass into the frame with brads or points at 3-inch intervals.
6. Put screw hooks into the top of the frame about an inch from each outer edge.
7. Hang in a window by a strong cord.

In summer, especially when the peaches appear on the table almost every day, a set of napkins made from a partly worn table cloth will be found a great savings of the best table linen; if hemmed neatly all around and then laundered as though they were real napkins, they look well for everyday use until the peach season is over; then if one examines these napkins and marks the many stains — for there will be a stain for every drop of peach juice spilled on them, until the frost comes to remove the spots — one will realize the great saving of good linen which has been accomplished.

"Uses for
Old Table Linens,"
House Beautiful, 1909

TALES OF OLD LACE

When people think of lace, a lot of them think of a demure little ruffle of white, snuggled around Granny's neck and secured by a cameo pin. But lace is, in fact, no tame textile. It has a long and decadent history. It has been an object of luxury and desire, coveted by some and outlawed by others. Sometimes it has been carefully regulated by kings and parliaments.

Lace came into being in Europe during the Renaissance as a simple ornamental border on undergarments. Skilled hands and minds improved and elaborated the methods of making lace until it became a textile so complex that the most expert worker could produce only a few inches of it a day. Lace was affordable only by the wealthy. Men and women of means sometimes wore ridiculous amounts of it. Cinq Mars, a French noble of the court of Louis XIII, owned three hundred pairs of trimmings for riding boots and as many

collars and pairs of cuffs. Members of the nobility sometimes wore more lace than they could afford, and some say that noblemen frequently ruined themselves with the enormous sums they paid for their lace. Laws were passed regulating what kind and how much lace a person of a particular rank might wear. In some American colonies, laws were passed prohibiting the wearing of lace altogether. Such vanity and frivolity were considered unsettling and even wicked by the somber New England patriarchs.

Lace was a problem for governments that were faced with huge sums of money flowing out of their treasuries into the coffers of the lacemaking centers of Europe. During one year in the reign of Louis XIV, more French francs were spent on Italian lace than on the entire French military. The government levied large import taxes on lace, making an already expensive item even more expensive. Lace was smuggled across borders. Sometimes dogs were caught crossing frontiers concealing lace in their collars. Something had to be done. Louis remedied this unfortunate state of affairs by importing a small army of Italian lacemakers to France to teach their secrets to the local folk. Within ten years, a large French lacemaking industry was established, and the national treasury looked much healthier. No doubt the Italians were furious.

The fortunes spent for lace supported a huge lacemaking population. Farmers' wives made lace in their spare time. Children made lace after, and sometimes instead of, school. Old ladies went blind making lace. Fishermen made lace in their off season. For several centuries, lace was a cash crop the European peasantry could depend upon.

Alencon Point

Bell Pattern Damascene Lace

Then the wearing of lace came to an abrupt halt in France. During the Reign of Terror, wearing anything the least reminiscent of the aristocracy was an incriminating link. A length of lace could cost you your head in those troubled times. The lacemakers starved, at least for a while.

Lace gradually returned to grace the gowns of great ladies, but it was never the fashion again for men. Nothing was considered so enticing as a flash of lace that graced a lady's bloomers. Frou-frou was in full bloom at the turn of the century. The impressionists record for us the frothy concoctions worn by ladies languishing in summer gardens or strolling

along the seaside. By this time, however, machines had taken over, and the exquisite handmade laces of centuries before were falling by the wayside. Although it was fashionable for leisured ladies to tat or crochet bits of lace, nothing so fine or exquisite was produced by these dilettante lacemakers as by those peasant women who went blind manipulating monumental numbers of bobbins for tiny wages. Handmade lace is now all but extinct.

In these times, bits of lace can be rescued from bins in thrift stores and flea markets. However, the new interest in anything old has made lace a collector's item again. But even so, an occasional treasure turns up. Antique stores often have fine examples that are sold for relatively small amounts, especially considering the time required to make even the most clumsy piece of crocheted lace. Collect it and marvel at these textiles that are mostly holes.

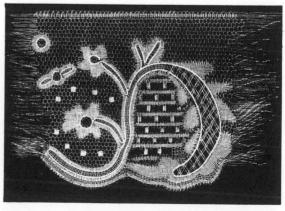

Bedford Regency Point

Badges

"I suppose that the oldest piece of cloth I have is my merit badge scarf from the Boy Scouts. I think I still have it; it's at home — if my mother didn't throw it away."

The author of this statement is a biophysicist in his mid-thirties. We know for a fact that he hates flea markets, abhors garage sales, and prides himself on regularly cleaning out his closet.

He doesn't save anything. But even the most unsentimental anti-pack rat among us can't part with his Boy Scout badges (and of course his mother still has them).

Badges are interesting, often very handsome bits of industrial embroidery. Collecting them can be fun. Thinking up something to do with them can be challenging.

DECORATE A JACKET WITH PLACES YOU HAVE BEEN.

FRAME THOSE BADGES.

DECORATE A VEST WITH SERGEANT STRIPES.

RAINBOWS

DISPLAY YOUR OLD MERIT BADGES OR DECORATE A BANNER WITH THEM.

COMPETITION QUILT WITH BADGES, PATCHES, AND APPLIQUES FROM THE OLD SCHOOL DAYS.

The Last Word on Rags

Once again I find myself at my sewing table. Before me lies a worn and colorless shirt, a bit of red satin, scraps of gold foil, an old turquoise top, two dingy gloves, a pack of deep blue dyestuff — the ingredients to transform a small boy into a fantastic superhero. Beside me is my trusty sewing machine. The task at hand is to change this old shirt into a bold uniform emblazoned with a brilliant red crest, to fashion the gold foil into a sash.

Even as the costume takes form I am aware of things to come. The approach of Christmas will lure these golden scraps from the drawer. The red satin will start to look like bows and sashes. It always happens.

In time all these fabrics will be reclaimed, some as humble mendings, others realizing stretches of my imagination. The ragbag is abundant and ever changing. As long as it continues to grow, I have only to dig deep into it for my fantasies to materialize.

Sew on and sew forth.

Stella Allison
October 30, 1978